D0217296

SWIMMING

About the Authors

Dr. Betty J. Vickers, a professor of physical education at Brigham Young University, Provo, Utah, has also taught at Kern Avenue Junior High School and University High School in Los Angeles, and at California State University at Northridge. She did her undergraduate study at Kent State University in Ohio where she started her competitive swimming experiences. Later, under the coaching of Mrs. Lilian MacKellar in Hollywood, California, she was twice the National AAU Solo Synchronized Swimming Champion and twice a member of the All American Synchronized Swimming Team. She represented the United States in the 1959 Pan American Games and received the Helm's Award for synchronized swimming in 1961. She did graduate work at California State University at Los Angeles where she received her Master of Arts in the fine arts in 1960. She earned an Ed.D. in physical education with an emphasis in philosophy from Brigham Young University in 1976. Miss Vickers is the author of four books and numerous articles in professional journals.

Dr. William J. Vincent is currently a professor in the Department of Kinesiology at California State University, Northridge. He received his doctorate from UCLA with special emphasis in the area of perception and motor learning and has had extensive experience in coaching gymnastics, swimming, and diving. From 1962 to 1969 he served as gymnastics coach and also coached the divers on the swim team. In 1968 and 1969, his gymnastics teams won the NCAA Division II Championships and he was named "Coach of the Year" in each case. Currently he teaches Measurement and Evaluation in Kinesiology, Computer Applications, and Quantitative Analysis of Research at CSUN. He is the author of two other books in the field of physical education and has published many articles in professional journals. Northridge, California, is home to Dr. Vincent where he resides with his wife Diana and six children.

SWIMMING
Sixth Edition

Betty J. Vickers
Brigham Young University

William Vincent
California State University/Northridge

Boston, Massachusetts   Burr Ridge, Illinios   Dubuque, Iowa
Madison, Wisconsin   New York, New York   San Francisco, California   St. Louis, Missouri

Book Team

Executive Editor *Ed Bartell*
Editor *Scott Spoolman*
Production Editor *Deborah J. Donner*
Visuals/Design Developmental Consultant *Marilyn A. Phelps*
Visuals/Design Freelance Specialist *Mary L. Christianson*
Publishing Services Specialist *Sherry Padden*
Marketing Manager *Pamela S. Cooper*
Advertising Manager *Jodi Rymer*

WCB/McGraw-Hill

A Division of The McGraw·Hill Companies

Executive Vice President/General Manager *Thomas E. Doran*
Vice President/Editor in Chief *Edgar J. Laube*
Vice President/Sales and Marketing *Eric Ziegler*
Director of Production *Vickie Putman Caughron*
Director of Custom and Electronic Publishing *Chris Rogers*

President and Chief Executive Officer *G. Franklin Lewis*
Corporate Senior Vice President and Chief Financial Officer *Robert Chesterman*
Corporate Senior Vice President and President of Manufacturing *Roger Meyer*

Consulting Editor
Physical Education
Aileene Lockhart
Texas Woman's University

Sports and Fitness Series Evaluation Materials Editor
Jane A. Mott
Texas Woman's University

Cover design by Regan Design

Cover image by Superstock/Four by Five

Copyedited by Karen Doland

Copyright © 1994 The McGraw-Hill Companies, Inc. All rights reserved

A Times Mirror Company

Library of Congress Catalog Card Number: 92–83886

ISBN 0–697–12664–1

No part of this publication may be reproduced, stored in a retrieval
system, or transmitted, in any form or by any means, electronic,
mechanical, photocopying, recording, or otherwise, without the
prior written permission of the publisher.

Printed in the United States of America by Wm. C. Brown Communications, Inc.,
2460 Kerper Boulevard, Dubuque, IA 52001

10 9 8 7 6 5 4 3 2

Contents

Standard Swimming Strokes   35

6

Beginning Diving   55

7

Special Water Activities   63

8

Conditioning   67

9

Preface

Swimming is a universally enjoyed, pleasurable activity. Its origins go back before any recorded history and, no doubt, many ancient people were accomplished swimmers. It is interesting to note that some of the earliest books ever published were on the subject of swimming. Nicholaus Wynman wrote a book in German on swimming in 1538,[1] and Melchiesedech Thevenot, a Frenchman, published a book titled "The Art of Swimming" in 1696.[2]

This activity serves many purposes: people learn to swim to survive, to search for food, to improve physical handicaps and health in general, to become safe in a foreign environment, to become capable of participating in other aquatic activities, and to swim for fun. Regardless of your purpose, the fundamental skills needed are the same. This little book was written to help speed your progress. Learn to swim well—respect the water—observe all precautions. If you do these things you will become safe and "at home" in the water and your enjoyment can be limitless.

Self-evaluation questions are distributed throughout these pages. These afford you typical examples of the kinds of understanding and levels of skill that you should be acquiring as you progress toward mastery of swimming. You should not only answer the printed questions but should pose additional ones as a self-check on learning. These evaluative materials are not necessarily positioned according to the presentation of given topics. In some instances you may find that you cannot respond fully and accurately to a question until you have read more extensively or have gained more experience. From time to time you should return to troublesome questions or to skill challenges until you are sure of the answers or have developed the skills called for, as the case may be.

A major reordering of the original material was made to make it more readable. The authors have written the book so that you can guide yourself from simple to complex skills. It was written for the person who begins as a non-swimmer and progresses through the various strokes. It also includes introductory information on elementary diving, water-related recreational sports, and competitive swimming and diving. You may progress through the book in order, or if you have already attained some skills, you may pick and choose the parts that are needed. We hope you will benefit from it and enjoy swimming as a lifelong, healthful, leisure-time activity.

1. Trustees of the British Museum, *British Museum Catalog of Printed Books to 1955,* Vol. 261 (London: Trustees of the British Museum, 1965).
2. Trustees of the British Museum, *British Museum Catalog of Printed Books to 1955,* Vol. 237 (London: Trustees of the British Museum, 1964).

Introduction

1

Through the ages swimming has become an extremely popular as well as a necessary skill. Once the fear of water is removed, most people experience a certain exhilarating feeling from submerging in water. Perhaps this feeling results from the water's cooling effect on a hot day, but more likely it results from that unique feeling of weightlessness produced by the buoyant action of the water. Absence of the normal pull of gravity can have a relaxing and tension-removing effect on your physical and mental state. For this reason, and for the wide recreational opportunities that the sport makes possible, thousands of people spend countless hours swimming.

The primary purpose of learning to swim is to make yourself at least reasonably secure when in or near the water. For this reason alone, everyone should learn to swim. Age does not appear to be a limiting factor to learning. Children have been known to swim before they can walk, and older folks use the water for its recreational and therapeutic values. In addition to the safety factors which are discussed in chapter 2, swimming offers enjoyment through unlimited recreational possibilities while concomitantly providing physiological and social values.

Values of Swimming

Physiological Values

Our hearts, lungs, muscles, and body systems need regular and vigorous exercise. Swimming contributes to the development and proper maintenance of most vital processes, and few activities contribute as much to the development of cardiovascular and respiratory fitness. Through swimming, most of the body's muscles are used, and by acting against the resistance of the water they gain strength. However, since swimming is primarily an endurance activity (the resistance is low but the repetition of movement is high), the cardiovascular system benefits more than the general muscular system.

The heart, vascular, and respiratory systems supply needed oxygen and nutriments to the body cells and carry away carbon dioxide and waste products. Maintaining a repeated activity such as a swimming stroke places a stress on this system which results in improvements of its ability to transport the materials in the bloodstream. Through the use of flotation devices and by varying the amount of energy put into the stroke, you can regulate the extent of the strain put on your system and thus reap the benefits desired. Improvement in cardio-vascular efficiency and the development of strength from moving against the resistance of the water is what is normally referred to as improving your physical fitness through swimming.

Recreational Values

Unprecedented advances in technology, science, medicine, and economics, have resulted in more people having more free time for fulfillment of creative self-expression. Knowing how to swim opens the door to countless recreational and leisure-time activities. By learning how to swim, one can contribute to present leisure needs while preparing for adventure in future aquatic activities.

It is no longer difficult to find facilities for most water sports. Billions of dollars are spent annually so that people can swim. Hotels, motels, resorts, and other forms of commercial establishments feature swimming as a prime activity to attract people for a night, weekend, or entire vacation time, and a private pool is now a feature of many homes.

Swimming opens up the frontier for new adventure and pleasure in the aquatic world. Recreational activities that you can enjoy after learning how to swim include competitive swimming, lifesaving and water safety methods, springboard diving, synchronized swimming, water shows, skin diving, scuba diving, surfboard riding, canoeing, motor boating, windsurfing, water skiing, sailing, fishing, aqua-aerobics, and other water games.

Social Values

Among the most important reasons for knowing how to swim are the social values that accrue. Swimming affords a splendid opportunity for youth and adults to participate together in healthy and natural aquatic activities. Because water sports are so diversified, many social groups in the form of aquatic clubs are organizing and holding periodic meetings throughout the year for the purpose of competition and socialization. Senior citizens and others often enjoy the benefits of aqua-aerobics through local recreation centers, retirement centers and spa or fitness centers. Water exercises with friends and neighbors can be enjoyed by everyone. Water exercises are wonderful for arthritics, those who are handicapped, women who are pregnant, athletes recovering from injury, and others who cannot participate in land-based physical activities. Swimming provides opportunities for the association of people from all parts of a community. It is one of the most popular family activities because all members of a family can play and recreate together.

Safety Values

It has been estimated that a large percentage of all persons who are drowned yearly are school-age children, and about half of these are engaged in a non-swimming water activity, such as boating, when drowning occurs. The safety values of being able to swim are of extreme importance. The ability to swim provides a great amount of insurance against possible mishap or tragedy.

For your own safety, as well as for the safety of your family and others, you should learn to swim. With the heavy increase in the number of aquatic facilities and equipment, both public and private, safety in and around water becomes a daily necessity. If you cannot swim it is extremely unwise to participate in most aquatic activities. The ability to swim safely and the prudence to recognize and practice safety procedures are of prime importance to you. Some hints on how these can be accomplished are offered in chapter 2.

Numerous lives were lost during recent wars through drownings. Many armed forces personnel were dumped into the water from amphibious landing craft during operations. In most cases the drownings that resulted could have been prevented if the troops had been able to swim, or in some instances, had been able only to tread water. Consequently the armed forces now spend considerable time and effort in teaching men and women to swim. The most effective way to reduce the number of swimming accidents is to teach everyone to swim, and to be a good and safe swimmer.

Special Values

Swimming is highly recommended by physicians for people with certain mental and physical disabilities. The buoyant force provided by the water allows a handicapped person to execute certain body movements that are impossible for him or her to perform otherwise. The handicapped person, the blind, the paralytic, the palsied, the crippled, and the person recovering from an injury may find the assistance, the outlet, and the physical exercise so urgently needed for improvement and recovery through swimming. Recent programs in aqua-aerobics have proven very successful in helping older or less active people find success in weight loss and cardiovascular conditioning.

Competitive Values

Most people are naturally competitive. You probably like to see how you compare with your friends in the performance of certain skills. Swimming offers you the opportunity to compete with others in many ways. Seeing who can swim the fastest or the farthest or with the best form, who can jump the highest off the board, who can make the biggest splash or the funniest dive are games that are enjoyed by many. Such natural outlets to this competitive drive will help you progress both physically and emotionally.

For those who desire even greater opportunity to compete, organized teams in schools and in private institutions are available.

What is the best form of insurance to protect against drowning accidents?

Equipment and Facilities

One of the aspects of swimming that makes it so universally enjoyable is the lack of expensive equipment. For more complicated activities such as water skiing and scuba diving, intricate equipment and specialized training are necessary; but for recreational swimming, all you need is a suit.

The suit can be obtained easily, but finding proper facilities that are both safe and sanitary may present a more difficult problem. In highly populated areas, public and private facilities are readily available to the interested participant. Just any old lake, stream or beach, however, may not be the best place to swim. Contaminated water, submerged rocks, or treacherous currents may be present, and such natural hazards should be thoroughly checked. But when these problems are eliminated, it is hard to top the pleasure of diving into the "old swimmin' hole."

The next chapter will review basic safety rules for swimming. Before you swim, read and think about the logic of these rules and how very important it is to follow them.

Lakes, ponds, rivers, and beaches may appear to be attractive swimming sites. What are the potential hazards you should check before venturing into unfamiliar waters?

Rules for Safety in Swimming

2

The general rules of swimming are concerned mostly with the safety of the participants. Most pools and public swimming areas post regulations that are designed to protect swimmers. Swimmers may neglect to observe these rules because they do not understand the reasons for their existence. Clarification of the "whys" of these rules might serve to improve both your interest in and willingness to observe them, and your efforts to see that others follow them as well.

1. Learn to swim well from a competent instructor.

   Why? Skill in swimming is the most effective way to save your life in a threatening situation involving water. A competent instructor can teach you skills, knowledge, and techniques that will help you deal appropriately with emergencies. It has been estimated that forty-seven percent of American adults do not know how to swim. This is an unfortunate statistic.

2. Never swim alone, regardless of your skill or experience.

   Why? That one time you are alone is when you might get a cramp, slip, be knocked unconscious, or meet with some unexpected problem that you cannot solve alone or that keeps you from seeking necessary assistance. It is just common sense to have a buddy while swimming.

3. Do not overestimate your ability.

   Why? Someone dares you to swim to an island in the middle of the lake. You are a strong swimmer, but when an unexpected storm comes up the waves are too much for you, or once you get out there, you are too tired to get back. There is always another day to surf, and the added safety factor of swimming long distances with a boat may keep you alive to do it again. The experts at channel swimming use a boat for their own safety even after years of conditioning. You certainly should do the same.

4. Never depend on air-filled flotation devices.

   Why? Deep-water swimming should be done by capable swimmers or under strict observation by an instructor while learning. If you are not able to take care of yourself under all unexpected circumstances, stay in the shallow area. Dependence on an air-filled inner tube or plastic float is just asking for trouble. When using a flotation device while in a water craft, make sure it is composed of solid material such as styrofoam.

5. Avoid strenuous swimming after eating.

   Why? Obviously a small snack such as a candy bar or hot dog will not affect your system greatly, but you should not enter into strenuous exercises of any kind right after eating a full meal. It would be just as unwise for you to play a strenuous tennis match or run in a track meet immediately after eating as it would be for you to swim. It is a common misconception that eating causes the blood to flow from your muscles to your stomach. Actually, during exercise the blood flow to the viscera is restricted so more can go to your muscles. Therefore, you can paddle around all you want on a full stomach, but hard swimming is not recommended until the food is digested.

6. Observe regulations involving limitations in swimming areas.

   Why? Lakes and oceans are marked with buoys to limit the safe swimming areas by experts who have screened the currents, undertows and marine life that may be harmful. Obviously, anyone who has ever been stung by a jelly-fish in the surf will be certain to observe the signs a second time. Additionally, the swimmer who has been caught in the kelp will stay out of that area. Being caught in overwhelming waves or currents however, might not let you have a second chance. Stay in the swimming area provided!

7. Always look before you jump or dive into a pool.

   Why? Of course none of us wants to jump on anyone, and diving on someone might prove fatal. In addition to these factors, it is terribly annoying to a beginner or an older person to be splashed or dunked as a result of horseplay. Common courtesy is the key factor in this case.

8. Only one diver on the board at one time.

   Why? It is lots of fun to break the spring of a friend who is about to take off into a "cannonball" causing him to land a little hard, but if you stand on the board when a novice is diving, that person might fall on the board or the deck and be severely injured. Do not take any chances. You would never forgive yourself if a friend of yours was severely injured as a result of your bad judgement.

9. No running on the pool deck.

   Why? This one should be obvious. The pool deck is slippery when wet.

10. Shower before entering the pool.

    Why? Here the concern is more for cleanliness and common decency than safety. The major purpose is to remove heavy oils like suntan lotion, greasy hair oil, or sand and dirt off your suit if you have been playing ball or sunning yourself. The pool can get pretty greasy and dirty if this rule is not observed when many people are swimming.

11. *Never attempt a swimming rescue when you are not qualified to do so,* and if you are a qualified lifeguard, swim after someone in distress only when there is *no* other means by which to give assistance. Time and time again we read this kind of headline in the daily newspaper: "Father Drowns Attempting to Save Son," "Two Men Die Rescuing Woman in Flood." How can this be prevented? Certainly a father cannot stand idly by while his son drowns, but there are many things that can be done other than swimming after the person. Two drownings are never better than one, and *if you are not qualified, do not swim out to give assistance.* Learn and practice this list instead: (reach, throw, row, go).

A. Reach

Get a pole, broom, or anything to extend your reach and assist the person in distress that way. Make a rope out of clothing, towels, or anything else nearby to extend the distance if the pole is not long enough. Once sufficient extension is secured, be certain that your base of support is low and firm so that you are not pulled into the water when the person in trouble grasps the pole.

Why? It takes much less time to gather extensions than it does to swim out, and if you have swum out too fast you will probably be too tired to be of any assistance once you get there. In addition, the fear factor will contribute to your ineffectiveness and rapid exhaustion.

B. Throw

Throw a rope, ring buoy, inner tube, or other object to the victim and pull him or her in, or wade out in shallow water to reach an extension to a person in distress. If you cannot reach the victim alone, form a "human chain" by linking wrists with others until you can reach or move out far enough to toss an extension. Again, be absolutely certain that the base of support is firm.

Why? In this way you can assist, whether you can swim or not, without endangering yourself.

C. Row

Use a boat if available, especially in natural water sites such as lakes or streams.

Why? It is faster and safer for both victim and rescuer, and unexpected water forces such as currents and undertows can be handled more easily.

D. Go

If you must swim to a victim, always take a buoy or other flotation device with you. Keep the flotation device well away from you as you extend it to the victim. Keep at least an arm's distance away so that you can freely swim back with the victim holding onto the buoy.

Why? Fear can make people do strange things, and being caught in a "strangle hold" is difficult even for a qualified lifeguard. Such a hold might prove fatal to you! Additionally, the flotation device can help support both you and the victim as you move towards safety. **Never** make a swimming rescue unless you are a qualified lifeguard!

12. Learn the basics of first aid and cardiopulmonary resuscitation (CPR). This book is not the appropriate place to learn all about these skills, so only a few introductory remarks will be made. You should seriously consider taking both a first aid and a CPR course from your local university, Red Cross, YMCA or YWCA. These skills can help you and others in many dangerous situations.

In order of choice what are the four methods for rescue of a swimmer in trouble? Name at least five objects that might be available at a beach or pool for extending your reach to a swimmer.

During an Accident

A brief assessment of the situation should be made in case of an accident. The few seconds it takes to check the injured person will assure appropriate action can be taken. If a person has sustained a neck or back injury such as falling from water skis or in a springboard diving mishap, more severe injury can be caused by moving the victim unnecessarily. A brief assessment will provide correct treatment or appropriate contact of professional aid with a minimum loss of time. When an accident occurs, keep the following steps in mind.

1. *Briefly assess the situation.* Check pulse and breathing. Do not move the victim if there is any possibility of neck or back injury.
2. *Send someone for help.* Most areas respond to the 911 emergency number.
3. *Administer CPR* if the victim has no pulse and you are certified. It is highly recommended that every adult become certified in administering both mouth-to-mouth resuscitation and CPR. Heart stoppage often accompanies accidents in and around water. Suffocation caused by drowning or electrocution is an example. Heart attack, stroke, and overuse of drugs are also common problems. If you are qualified, you can add CPR to your ability to help in emergency situations. It may be the means of saving the life of a member of your family or one of your friends.
4. *Administer mouth-to-mouth resuscitation* if the person has stopped breathing. Never administer artificial respiration to someone who is breathing. Ask the victim if he or she is "OK." A person who can respond is breathing.
5. *Treat for shock.* Keep the victim warm. Elevate feet if the victim can be moved and there is no injury to the head. Do not change the position of a person who has a neck or back injury unless death is imminent if you do not move them.

Mouth-to-Mouth Resuscitation

If a person has stopped breathing immediate action should be taken. Be sure to ask if the victim is "OK." If the victim responds, he or she must be breathing. Administering artificial respiration when a person is breathing, even shallowly, can cause the victim to stop breathing.

If the victim has collapsed without physical injury, turn the victim onto his or her back. If there has been an injury on the diving board or from another violent accident, use your own judgment in moving the person. The best method for turning is to support the victim's head with one hand while you roll the person onto his or her back by drawing the shoulder and hip toward you in one smooth motion. Try to keep the body from twisting.

Open the airway of the victim by tilting the head back with one hand on the forehead, and the other pulling the jaw forward. This keeps the tongue from blocking the air passage (fig. 2.1). Recheck for breathing with the head in this position. Look to see if the chest is rising as you place your ear near the mouth to hear and feel for the victim's breathing.

If the victim is not breathing, give two slow, full breaths to inflate the lungs completely. Squeeze the victim's nose and form a seal by placing your mouth over the victim's mouth to blow into the lungs. Be sure that a tight seal is formed. Check the victim again for breathing.

If the victim is still not breathing, begin artificial respiration. A full breath should be given every five seconds with a rest after each breath to allow lungs to fill. Count to yourself by saying, "Breathe-one thousand, two-one thousand, three-one thousand, four-one thousand, five-one thousand, breathe-one thousand. . . ." etc. Be sure that the victim's chest is rising with each breath and falling when you remove your mouth to inhale again (fig. 2.2).

Sometimes the victim's stomach will inflate during artificial respiration. This air may be expelled by pressing gently on the victim's stomach. Since this action may cause the victim to vomit, be sure to clear the air passage by turning the head to the side and clearing the mouth with the forefinger. Resume administering artificial respiration and continue until help arrives.

Mouth-to-mouth resuscitation may also be administered to an infant and a small child in a similar manner. First, check for breathing and pulse. Give two slow breaths, but blow only the air from your cheeks into an infant. If the infant is still not breathing, begin artificial respiration. Seal both the mouth and the nose with your mouth as you blow. A small puff of air should be given every three seconds. Release your mouth and watch the baby's chest fall as you inhale. Be sure that only small puffs of air are given to an infant as powerful exhalations from an adult could burst the lungs of an infant or small child.

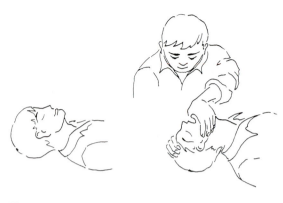

Figure 2.1
Head tilt to free air passage.

Figure 2.2
Mouth-to-mouth resuscitation.

Key Points to Remember

1. Assess the situation.
2. Ask if the victim is "OK." Check pulse and breathing.
3. Send someone for help.
4. Tilt head back to clear air passage.
5. Look, listen, and feel for breathing.
6. Give two slow, full breaths to inflate lungs.
7. Re-check breathing and pulse.
8. Administer mouth-to-mouth resuscitation.
   A. One breath every five seconds per adult.
   B. One small breath every three seconds per infant.
9. Continue administering artificial respiration until help arrives.

In what ways does the technique of administering mouth-to-mouth resuscitation to an adult differ from administering it to an infant or small child?

Cardiopulmonary Resuscitation

CPR or cardiopulmonary resuscitation is a method of external heart massage that may prevent death when a person's heart has stopped beating. Possible causes of heart failure include a stroke, heart attack, suffocation, electric shock, or drugs.

The administration of CPR must be correct and efficient or severe injury can result. CPR should never be practiced on another healthy person. Practice should only be done on a mannequin or other artificial substitute for a human subject.

Because of the dangers involved, this procedure should be learned only under the careful supervision of qualified instructors. The American Red Cross will provide expert instruction to any adequately large group upon request. Classes are also offered at regular intervals for individuals desiring to become certified. It is strongly recommended that every adult become certified in the administration of CPR. It's the least expensive life insurance you can obtain.

Call your local Red Cross office now to enroll in a class of CPR.

Swimming, like any other sport, has its own nomenclature. Chapter 3 contains a brief history of swimming and a glossary of terms. As you progress through the book, refer to it often to assure yourself that you understand the correct meaning of new terms.

A Brief History of Swimming and a Definition of Terms

3

The word "swimming" is derived from the Old English term "swimmin."[1] Although the origin of swimming is not really known, people probably learned how to swim from watching animals. Mosaics unearthed in Pompeii show men navigating water under their own power, and a bas-relief in a tomb from the 2000 B.C. period in Egypt shows a swimmer doing what appears to be a crawl stroke.

The English were the first people of modern times to compete in swimming as a sport rather than using it primarily as a skill for survival. Records show that competitive swimming began about 1837 in London. Early English swimmers used the breaststroke and the sidestroke.

In 1844 North American Indians entered a swimming meet in London. Flying Gull defeated Tobacco by swimming the length of a 130-foot pool in thirty seconds. The style of swimming used by the Indians was similar to a windmill action. Each arm thrashed the water violently in a circular motion while the feet beat the water in an up-and-down action. This type of action was a form of the crawl stroke.

Most early swimming consisted primarily of the breaststroke and some side-stroking. In 1873, J. Arthur Trudgen introduced an overhand stroke using the scissors kick which was to become known as the "trudgen crawl." Using the trudgen crawl, J. H. Derbyshire swam 100 yards in sixty seconds for the world record. This stroke has recently been restored to competitive swimming, and some modern distance swimmers have set new records using it.

In 1878, Frederick Cavill, an Englishman, went to Australia. After observing that the natives' flutter kick leg action resulted in exceptional speed, he combined it with the double overhand stroke. This stroke became known as the "Australian crawl." Cavill set a new world record of 58.4 seconds for 100 yards in the 1902 world championships using this stroke. About 1905, Charles M. Daniels, a swimmer for the New York Athletic Club, introduced the "American crawl" and used it to set a world record of 54.8 seconds in the 100 yard swim in 1910. The only difference between the "Australian crawl" and the "American crawl" was that in the American crawl the kick was timed to the stroking of the arms—six beats of the legs for every revolution of the arms. At the time of this writing, the world record for the 100 meter free-style (front

---

1. For further information on swimming history consult: American Red Cross, *Swimming and Diving*, (St. Louis: C.V. Mosby Co., 1992). David A. Armbruster, Robert H. Allen, and Hobert S. Billingsley, *Swimming and Diving* 7th ed. (St. Louis: C.V. Mosby Co., 1979).

crawl) is 48.42 seconds, set by American Matt Biondi, on August 10, 1988. The American Red Cross first published a nationwide water safety program which had been developed by Wilbert E. Longfellow in 1914. This plan and others since have reduced the drowning rate in this country from 10.4 per 100,000 in 1914 to 1.9 per 100,000 in 1990.

Glossary of Terms

The following definitions may be helpful to you in understanding the terminology of water sports.

Approach and hurdle
The walking steps (approach) and the jump (hurdle) to the end of the springboard in diving. Competitively, the approach must contain at least four steps which includes the hurdle. The hurdle consists of lifting one leg up until the thigh is parallel to the board and the lower leg is perpendicular to the board, jumping off of the supporting foot and landing on both feet.

Aqua-aerobics
The performance of aerobic exercise activities in waist- or chest-deep water to take advantage of water resistance and buoyancy, and to prevent damage to the joints in the lower extremities.

Aquatics
Pertaining to water or to activities performed in water.

Archimedes' principle
An object immersed in a medium is buoyed up by a force equal to the weight of the volume of the medium displaced. Usually the medium is water, but it could be any liquid or gas. A balloon floats in air because it weighs less than the volume of the air it displaces. Your body floats in water because you weigh less than the water you displace. If you truly cannot float, then you weigh more than the water you displace.

Buoyancy
The upward force of water on a submersed object. See Archimedes' principle.

Butterfly
A relatively new stroke used in competition and considered the second fastest stroke. The arms work in a crawl action, but both hit the water and pull at the same time. The kick is a dolphin kick similar to the flutter, but both feet kick up and down together at the same time.

Cardiopulmonary resuscitation—CPR
A means of external heart massage that may be used to revive persons experiencing heart failure.

Finning
An action of the arms like the fins of a fish, resulting mostly from the movement of the elbow and the wrist in and out from the body, in a press and recovery action.

Float

To be suspended in the water.

a. *Tuck float.* To float with your hips and knees flexed and with your hands holding your shins, with your head down in the water, and your rounded back bobbing above the surface.

b. *Prone float.* To float face down with arms and legs extended.

c. *Supine float.* To float face up. Position of arms and legs, and the degree of horizontal or vertical positioning is determined by the density of the floater's body.

Glide

a. A period in which the body is moving in an extended position as a result of prior propulsion through the water.

b. The resting phase of the breast, elementary back, and sidestrokes. The body is floating and gliding through the water as a result of the last kick or pull of the arms.

Gutter

The edge of the pool at water level. Water from the surface splashes over the gutter and is drained away. This helps keep the water surface clean and less agitated.

Hurdle

See approach and hurdle.

Kick

To propel the body through the water with the legs.

a. *Dolphin.* Both legs moving up and down together.

b. *Flutter.* Both legs moving up and down alternately.

c. *Scissors.* A bending of the knees and extension of the legs forward and backward in relation to the body, then a hard squeeze to a stretch position. Probably the most powerful but not the fastest kick. While lying on the side in the water, if the top leg extends forward it is called the regular scissors kick, but if the top leg extends backward it is called the inverted scissors kick. The inverted kick is used for certain lifesaving techniques.

d. *Whip.* A recovery or power kick in which the knees are bent as the ankles are flexed, and the toes are rotated outward on the recovery, then the feet and legs press out and down into extension on the power phase.

Mouth-to-mouth resuscitation

A form of artificial respiration that may be used to revive a person who has stopped breathing.

Natatorium

A building where swimming and other water activities take place.

Newton's third law of motion

For every action made in the water there is an equal and opposite reaction which propels the body through the water.

Personal floatation device—PFD

A device designed to support a person in the water such as a water ski vest, or boating life jacket.

Pike

A body position with the knees straight, the hips bent, and the back rounded. The arms may be touching the legs or extended out to the side.

Pull

An action of the arms imparting force on the water toward the body to propel a person through the water.

Push

An action of the arms or legs that propels a person through the water by imparting force on the water away from the body.

Recovery phase

That part of a stroke in which the arms or legs have thrust the body through the water and are now returning to the position for another thrust.

Resistance or drag

The greater the surface area that is presented to the water, the greater the resulting resistance or ''drag'' on the body.

Scuba

Self-contained underwater breathing apparatus. Usually an air tank strapped to the back and connected to the mouth by a flexible tube and mouthpiece.

Sculling

A means of propelling oneself through the water with the hands and forearms executing a figure-eight action. Constant pressure is exerted on both the in and out phases of the arm action.

Snorkeling

To explore and dive in water using a face mask, a snorkel tube, and swim fins.

Snorkel tube

A tube, usually about a foot long, going from the mouth to just above the surface of the water. The swimmer breathes through the tube.

Stretch

To extend the body into a straight line with arms and legs extended, toes pointed, and back straight.

Stroke

A complete cycle of the arms and legs in a coordinated manner to propel a person through the water. Sometimes this term refers only to the arm action of the total movement.

Surfing

To swim or glide with the waves at the beach and let them carry you to the shore. Board surfing consists of standing, kneeling, or sitting on a long board and riding the waves to shore. Body surfing uses only the body and no board.

Synchronized swimming

A form of swimming in which competitors perform various strokes and water gymnastic figures to music. Many of the figures are extremely difficult to accomplish. Competitors in this sport are judged on their form, execution, style, originality, and the difficulty of the figures.

Tuck

A body position with the knees bent, the hips bent, and the chest on the knees. The hands are usually holding on to the shinbones. The head may be tilted forward or backward.

Water skiing

A sport in which a person is pulled over the water by a boat while standing on wood or fiberglass planks called skis. The skis have rubber bindings to hold the feet to the skis.

Windsurfing

The act of standing on a surfboard equipped with a sail and sailing over the water propelled by wind.

What do the initials "PFD" stand for? Name some examples.

Beginning Techniques for the Nonswimmer

4

If you have a fear of the water, these techniques will help you. Take them slowly, one at a time. Not all people have an initial fear of water however. Indeed, some children have to be held back before they are safe near pools or oceans. Whether you are fearful or not, the best way to approach swimming for the first time is slowly and rationally with some time-honored techniques that are used by all well-qualified instructors.

Entering the Water

Your first contact with the water for swimming may be somewhat unsettling. Pool or natural water is usually cooler than bathwater, and contact with it may cause several reactions. The most common of these is the noticeable tenseness and tightening of your muscles. Your skin may shrivel up slightly and you may get "goose pimples." When you submerge to chest depth, your breathing becomes more difficult. This is due mostly to the tenseness of the musculature needed in breathing. In addition, you might notice a quickening of your pulse. The strange feeling of buoyancy also begins to take effect at this point. This may produce a very exhilarating feeling and can cause some laughter and desire to let yourself bob a little. Don't be afraid to let yourself go. Enjoy this feeling, for it is one of the unique pleasures of swimming.

If the water seems too cold at first, don't go in all the way. Stand about knee deep and splash some water on your arms, trunk, neck, and head. This will help you become accustomed to the change in temperature, and submersion will then not seem to be so drastic.

Relaxing in the Water

Once you are in the water, the next step is to feel relaxed in it. If you can find a spot where the water is only about two feet deep, sit on the bottom and let your feet float up in front of you. Keep your hands down to balance your new-found weightlessness and try moving around. Use slow easy movements in the water. Because water is more dense than air, you can't move about as quickly. Take your time and think of moving in slow motion. This will help you to relax. Roll over from your back to your face and vice versa. Let the back of your head dip into the water while you keep your hands on the bottom, and then let your legs and trunk drift up into a float with your back almost parallel to the bottom. Turn over and try the same thing in a prone position.

Submerging

After you begin to feel relaxed in the water, try putting your head underwater. Duck just a little at first so that your nose and mouth are submerged. Hold your breath for a few seconds and come up. Next, put your whole head beneath the surface, hold the position for a few seconds, and then surface. Try to resist the temptation to wipe your eyes with your hands. This is a bad habit to get into, as later on it will inhibit your progress. Good technique in swimming requires your eyes to be open most of the time. Since you can't wipe them while swimming, you must learn to open them and let the water run off naturally. The water in which you are swimming is much cleaner than the water you drink from a faucet. Some water will get in, of course, but it will not hurt. You will become used to it, and later on you will not even be aware of it.

The next time you go under, open your eyes slightly. The sight you see will be most interesting. Other swimmers in brightly colored suits, the bottom of the pool, and your own body will greet your eyes in a blurry but beautiful scene. The blur results from the changed angle of refraction between the water and your eyes. This angle is different from that which occurs between the air and your eyes. Blur can be corrected by wearing a diving mask. You may want to try this. With it the same beautiful picture emerges in crystal clarity. Imagine seeing fish, seaweed, shells, and other sea life in this setting. No wonder snorkeling and scuba diving have become so popular!

Have a partner or your instructor hold out several fingers under the water while you go under and count them, or drop some coins in the water and dive down to the bottom and pick them up. These two drills will demonstrate to you your ability to see under water and will help you become accustomed to your new environment. One caution about coins, however—don't leave them on the bottom as they will stain the pool. The same rule applies to hairpins and other metallic objects that rust.

Breath Control

Breath control—that ability to hold your breath and release it gradually or rapidly, to exhale, to gasp air, or inhale quickly—is difficult to develop, but it is essential for maximum success in water activities. Nature did not endow people with the apparatus to convert the oxygen in water to suitable use for the body. Diving tanks, aqualungs, snorkels, and the like have been developed to sustain life in and under water for long periods of time. Success in the use of such equipment and water activities without them however, depends upon your individual breath control.

Holding your breath is the first step. Take a deep breath and submerge; hold it for a few seconds, then surface. The next time try counting to ten, then twenty, and finally thirty. When you reach forty-five, you have good breath control. You will find that thinking of something else while underwater will make it easier to hold your breath.

Make sure you do not try staying under too long—about thirty seconds should be the maximum length of time. If you find it difficult to keep yourself under the surface, "fin" by pressing toward the surface with the palms of your hands held out to your sides. This finning action is a simple press with your palms up and a recovery with your wrists relaxed. Your hands are drawn down the sides, and then pressed upward toward the surface, with your fingertips pointing out and away from your body. Repeat this action in a short, rapid rhythm.

Bobbing

Breath control is not limited to breath holding. You must develop the ability to breathe in and out according to the head actions of the stroke you are performing. The first rhythmic breathing method to practice is called bobbing. Begin to learn bobbing by holding on to the side of the pool in about chest-deep water. By bending your knees and straightening them, bob up and down holding your breath the whole time. Make the rhythm of the bob even and try to break the surface about every four or five seconds. After you have mastered this, take a breath of air, submerge and blow all of your air out in about two seconds. Then try it again—inhale, submerge, and exhale so that it now takes five seconds to get it all out. Repeat this exercise varying the length of time you take to exhale completely so that you can do it at any rate required. Exhale through both your mouth and nose. Do not hold your nose.

Bobbing can and should be practiced in many positions. For example, try it while holding a kickboard or while a partner holds your hands. You should also practice explosive exhalation by bobbing and forcefully blowing out all of your air at once under water. In doing this, do not change the rhythm of the bob, only the speed of exhalation. Practice until you can inhale and exhale at any rate and still feel comfortable. Slow, controlled exhalation is usually preferred, but sometimes you will need to exhale quickly, so learn to do both. Now standing in chest-deep water, combine the exhalation with a rapid inhalation. Assume the bobbing position (fig. 4.1), inhale, submerge, exhale, and surface at the two-second rate. Time your breathing so that you always exhale when you are under water and inhale when you are above. At first you will be able to make only about three or four cycles before you have to break the rhythm to take a few breaths above the surface. Keep practicing until you can go on indefinitely at your normal breathing rate with complete confidence and comfort.

While bobbing, don't be alarmed if some water enters your mouth. It will not go back beyond your tongue unless you swallow or suck it in while you inhale. Let it pool up in your cheeks or under your tongue and simply expel it

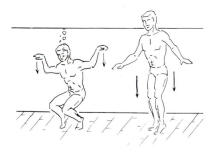

Figure 4.1
Bobbing is one way to practice rhythmic
breathing.

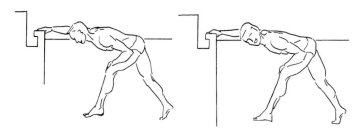

Figure 4.2
Rhythmic breathing for swimming.

with the next exhalation. One of the skills that has to be mastered in this bobbing technique is the separation of the air from the water in your mouth, and
with practice this will come naturally. A modification of bobbing can be developed into a drown-proofing technique. This will be explained in detail in
chapter 5.

Rhythmic Breathing for Swimming

You are now ready to begin developing rhythmic breath control for swimming
strokes. Standing in waist-deep water in a stride position, one leg forward and
one leg back, hold on to the side of the pool and lean over so that your upper
body is resting on the surface of the water (fig. 4.2). Extend the arm that is
holding on to the wall and hold the other back down at your side. Take a
breath, place your face in the water so that the water level is at your hairline,
and exhale. Turn your face to the side, away from the extended arm, just far
enough to inhale through the mouth. Then turn the face back down and exhale
through the mouth and nose. Continue this action, breathing rhythmically, as
before. Keep your eyes open and your ear in the water while inhaling, and
neither shake nor rub the water out of your eyes while practicing. This type of
rhythmic breathing will be used later in the crawl stroke.

Moving in the Water

So far all the techniques have been in a static position. To navigate properly, you must propel yourself through the water. Always practice the following skills in shallow water. Begin by walking in about waist-deep water. Because of the density of the water, you will find that you cannot go very fast. Lean forward and draw your hands and arms back as if separating a curtain of water before you to help pull yourself through the water. Reach forward with both hands in front of you, then turn the palms and thumbs down and out to pull your hands and forearms through the water sideways back to your hips. This is much like the breaststroke pull and it increases your speed in walking considerably. Experiment with your hands by pulling and pushing in various directions. Discover how to turn your body clockwise and counterclockwise with your hands. Jump and do a full pirouette and come down on your feet. If you should go under, surface again as you did in rhythmic breathing practice.

Now go into the water about chest deep with a kickboard and hold it out in front of you with both hands. Bend your knees and push forward slightly so that your feet come off the bottom and you are supported only by the board. Glide or float for a few seconds and then return your feet to the bottom. If your legs float up and won't come down, bend your knees and hips so that your knees come up under your chest, push down on the board while lifting your head, extend your legs and feet straight toward the bottom, and stand up.

Flutter Kicking

The kick used most often in swimming is the flutter kick. You can practice it while holding onto the side of the pool. Place one hand on the gutter of the pool and the other about one foot deep against the side. With the palm against the side point the fingers of this hand down toward the bottom. By pulling with the top hand and pushing with the bottom one, raise your feet and legs up until they are parallel to and just under the surface of the water. Begin kicking your whole leg up and down from the hip joint. Do not forcibly bend your knees or ankles, but keep them loose. When your leg kicks down, the knee will bend from the water pressure, and when you kick up, it will straighten from the pressure. Try to imitate the relaxed leg feeling you get when walking at a leisurely rate. As you progress you can forcibly extend your knee at the end of the downstroke, but at the beginning keep it loose so that you will develop the proper technique. Let the ankles stay as loose as possible and point your toes inward very slightly so that you feel a little pigeon-toed. Let the water flop your feet up and down like swim fins. Your foot should be about eighteen inches below the surface at its lowest point, and your heel should just break the surface at the top of the kick. Count your kicks in a six-stroke rhythm (fig. 4.3).

Figure 4.3
Flutter kick practice.

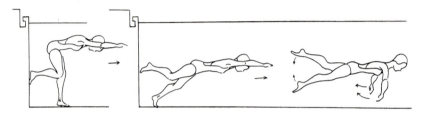

Figure 4.4
Underwater swimming.

When gliding face down with a kickboard, your legs may not drop down automatically when you want to stand up. How should you move to recover an upright position easily?

While you are holding onto the side and kicking, practice your rhythmic breathing by turning your head sideways to inhale and turning your head down to exhale. Keep your head in such a position that the water level hits you at the hairline when you are exhaling, and your ear is submerged with the water level just below the mouth when you are inhaling. Add this rhythmic breathing and the flutter kick to your float, or glide with the kickboard so that you propel yourself across the pool.

Swimming Under Water

Another skill that sounds hard but is really easy to learn is swimming under water. Once you have learned breath control, the flutter kick, and the long breaststroke pull that was used in walking through the water, you are ready to swim under water. Stand with your back against the side of the pool and submerge. Put one foot up against the side of the pool, both hands stretched out in front of you, and push off into a prone position about two feet under the surface of the water. Kick your feet vigorously, using the flutter kick or another substituted kick, while you pull your hands and forearms back to your hips as before. You will probably go only about five or six feet the first time, but your distance may be increased by repeating the pull and continuing your kick. Open your eyes and count the lines on the bottom of the pool as you swim past them (fig. 4.4).

All of the foregoing skills may be simple for you to learn, so progress at the rate which is comfortable for you. Do not go on to a new stage until the prior skill is accomplished, but move as quickly as you can and listen to the hints and directions given by your teacher. Do not force yourself to attempt deep-water stunts or any other activities for which you do not feel prepared. When you think you should progress to another skill, ask your instructor and then follow his or her advice. When these basic skills have been accomplished and you have become accustomed to the water, you are ready to go on to regulation swimming strokes and techniques.

Basic Swimming Skills

5

Skills for swimming are varied and numerous, and a good swimmer will master all of them because a well-rounded swimmer is accomplished in even the most basic water skills.

Floating

The first essential skill is floating. Although the technique involved is natural to many, it is not to all. Everyone, however, can learn either the skill of motionless floating or of floating with minimal kicking and finning. There are three common positions in which a person can float. The first is called the tuck—this type of float can best determine your capacity to float. The prone or face float is the second type and is the beginning position for all strokes performed on the stomach or face. The third type of float is the supine or back float. Floating on the back is more difficult for most people, but control in this position is an essential prerequisite to performance of all strokes done on the back.

Whether or not an object floats in water is determined by its density. Since water is a universal substance, it has arbitrarily been given a density of 1.00. If a given volume of another material weighs more than an equal volume of water, it has a density greater than 1.00. Thus it will sink when placed in water. If the material weighs less than an equal volume of water, it has a density of less than 1.00. Thus it will float. For example, wood has a density of less than 1.00, so it floats, but a brick has a density of greater than 1.00 and, therefore, sinks.

Typically, the human body has a density slightly less than 1.00. A few people, however, have densities greater than 1.00. These people cannot float motionlessly, but that does not mean they are unable to swim. They cannot, however, float without some form of arm or leg motion to provide an upward force. These "sinkers," as they are often called, usually become very good swimmers because they have learned to effectively use their arms in skills such as sculling and their legs in many forms of kicking to keep themselves afloat. In addition to the propelling force, when a body moves through the water, there is a planing effect that tends to lift a body up. This lifting effect comes from the force of moving water on the chest or back. It is the same force that lifts a speedboat up in the water as it begins to move fast.

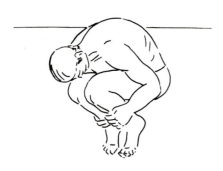

Figure 5.1
The tuck float.

To test your ability to float, execute a tuck float. If your feet come off the bottom of the pool and your back remains at the surface, your density is less than 1.00. If you sink to the bottom, your density is greater than 1.00. Most true "sinkers" are heavily muscled with little fatty tissue.

Many centuries ago the Greek philosopher Archimedes discovered the principle of flotation when he declared, "An object immersed in a medium is buoyed up by a force equal to the weight of the volume of the medium displaced." Fresh water weighs 62.4 pounds per cubic foot. Therefore, if an object has one cubic foot of volume, it will be buoyed up by a force of 62.4 pounds when submerged in water. If an object, such as a brick, weighs more than 62.4 pounds in air, it will sink. It will however, weigh 62.4 pounds less under water than it does in air. If the object weighs less than 62.4 pounds in air, it will float in water.

This explains why it is easier to float in the ocean or salt water than it is in fresh water. Since seawater weighs 64 pounds per cubic foot of volume, it buoys up objects with more force than does fresh water.

You can change your body density by filling your lungs with air, thus increasing your total body volume. This reduces your density so you can float. Most floaters can become sinkers by changing the volume of their body. Take a large breath of air and hold it while floating in a tuck position; now exhale as much air as you can. You will probably sink. By decreasing the volume of your chest when you exhaled the air, you changed your density from slightly less than 1.00 to slightly more than 1.00.

Flotation techniques can also be used to estimate the volume of the human body. If a person has neutral buoyancy (just barely floats), or in other words has a density of 1.00, and that person weighs 125 pounds, then the volume of his body is about 2 cubic feet, ($2 \times 62.4 = 124.8$).

The Tuck Float

To determine your ability to float try the tuck float. Stand in chest-deep water, take a deep breath of air, and hold it in your lungs. Reach down and grasp your ankles while pulling your knees toward your chest (fig. 5.1). Let your head hang comfortably into the water. If your feet come off the bottom of the pool

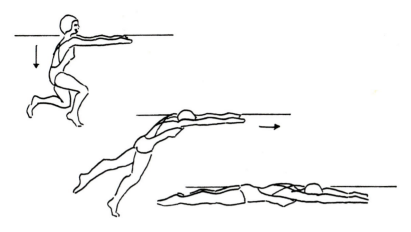

Figure 5.2
Prone float and guide.

and your back remains at the surface, you can float. The degree to which you can float however, varies with each individual. To return to a standing position, sweep your arms in a circular motion out to the sides, then forward and downward. This action should depress your feet and lift your head. Extend your feet to the bottom of the pool and stand up. Open your eyes and let the water run off your face.

Prone Float and Glide

Once the tuck float is accomplished, the prone or face float becomes relatively easy. From a standing position in chest-deep water, extend both arms out in front of your body and stoop until your shoulders are under water (fig. 5.2). Take a deep breath and place your face into the water. Lean gently forward, push off the wall with one foot, and let your legs and feet come off the bottom of the pool. Glide in this position until you stop moving. To stand up, draw your hands and arms back to your sides and down toward the bottom in a circular motion. At the same time, draw your knees to your chest and then extend your feet to the bottom of the pool.

What change must you make in your normal breathing pattern to avoid getting water in your nose as you float or swim?

Supine Float

The supine or back float is perhaps the most difficult to learn because water may be splashed over the face and nose, and beginners often become tense when this happens.

Again, start by standing in chest-deep water with one foot forward and one foot back. Stoop until the water is over your shoulders and extend your arms out to the sides at shoulder height (fig. 5.3). Take a deep breath and lay your head back in the water until your ears are submerged. Now lift your chest and

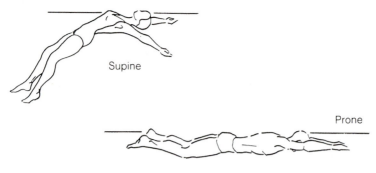

Figure 5.3
Floating.

allow your body to level off on your back. Keep your chest and stomach up. Do not sit in the water. Make no attempt to get your feet to the surface. Most people will float in a semivertical position on their backs. You may need to extend your arms overhead to find a balance point, but be sure to keep them under the water. If you had some trouble floating in the tuck position, you may need to scull or kick slightly, but relax and try to hold this basic position for maximum floating effectiveness with minimum effort.

Balance is the main problem in the back float. Be sure that your arms are stretched well out to the side, or well overhead as needed, and that your chest and stomach are held high. Scull or kick only if it is absolutely necessary. Try holding the back float without assistance. To return to a standing position, sit in the water by raising your head and dropping your hips. At the same time scoop your arms back, down, and forward in a circular motion and draw your knees to your chest. Then extend your feet toward the bottom.

If you have some difficulty in floating on your back, you may find that it is helpful to allow your heels to drop down in the water. This slight knee bend is quite natural for those that are less buoyant. Very few people float with their entire body, legs, and feet at the surface of the water.

Sculling

A means of propelling or supporting yourself in the water using only the hands and forearms in a figure-eight motion is called sculling. This technique is a particularly effective tool to use in assisting yourself in floating on your back, in learning or practicing kicking skills on your back, for treading water, and for controlling your movements in underwater position changes.

Swimming on the Surface

Prone Glide and Flutter Kick

The prone or face float and glide with a flutter kick is the first step toward learning swimming strokes. From the fully extended prone float position, the up-and-down flutter kick is added to propel the body across the pool. To do the flutter kick, you should keep your legs relatively straight but relaxed so there is some bend at the knee. The kick should be about eighteen inches deep and rather fast (about three kicks per second). Your legs should move in an action similar to that used for walking except that the ankles are extended. Your feet and legs should be kept under water throughout the kick with no more than your heel breaking the surface at any point. Greater flexibility in the ankle will produce a more powerful kick, provided all other aspects are correctly performed. (Review chapter 4 for flutter kick practice.)

To add this kick to the prone float, stand in chest-deep water with your shoulders under the surface and extend your arms out in front of your body. Take a deep breath and place your face in the water so that the water level is at your hairline, gently push off the bottom into a prone position, and kick from the hips—this action will propel your body across the water. It may be necessary to link your thumbs to keep your hands together. Try to stretch your body in as long a line as possible for maximum success.

Supine Float and Flutter Kick

The supine or back float and flutter kick should be the first step toward learning strokes on your back, and it should be practiced early in the learning experience. Too often swimmers learn only prone swimming so the transition to other positions is difficult.

What is the movement pattern of the hands and arms in sculling? Can you propel yourself across the pool in supine position by sculling?

The flutter kick on the back is similar to the flutter kick on the face with a strong emphasis on the up action of the kick. Again, the legs should be kept relatively straight but relaxed with the toes and ankles extended. There should be some knee bend, and the kick should be deep and rather fast. Be sure not to sit in the water but to keep your trunk as straight and level as possible.

Adding the flutter kick to the back float is much like adding the kick to the prone float. From a standing position in chest-deep water, stoop to submerge your shoulders, extend your arms overhead, and place your head and arms back in the water. Take a deep breath, gently push off the bottom into a supine float position, and kick from the hips, thus propelling your body across the pool.

Finning

The back float and flutter kick may be performed with your arms at the sides rather than overhead. The arms at the sides position is easier, but the arms overhead position encourages a better body line for future stroke development. Until sufficient strength is developed, it may be necessary for you to add a finning motion with your hands while working on this kick. Finning is performed by drawing your hands up at the sides of your body and then pushing the palms down toward the feet. It is an alternating press and recovery action. Both hands are drawn up simultaneously and the press results from a whipping action of your hands and forearms with your fingertips pointing out. Thus, the press is toward the feet and propels the body headfirst. Be sure to keep your eyes open and your breathing as regular as possible.

Turning Over from Prone to Supine Positions

After the supine float with flutter kick and the prone float with flutter kick have been learned, it is important to learn to roll from the back to the face and vice versa so that it is not necessary for you to stop swimming in order to take a breath. Start the prone float and flutter kick with your arms out in front (fig. 5.4). When you wish to roll onto your back, turn your head and draw your shoulder and hip back at the same time. This action will cause you to roll over, and you can continue on using the supine float with the flutter kick. To return to the face down position, simply turn your head into one arm and raise your opposite hip and shoulder—you will roll over. If you are still unsuccessful, bring one leg over the other one to complete the turn and go right on kicking. It would help to practice this turning on land before attempting it in the water. When this skill is accomplished, your fears should be nearly overcome.

Your head controls the direction of your body in the water. How should you move your head to turn from the prone to the supine position? How should you move your head to return to the face down position?

Treading Water

The skill of treading water is one that all swimmers should master, and it is mandatory for participation in the strenuous sport of water polo. This skill is also essential for safety so that you can maintain yourself in the water after a spill, such as in water skiing or boating. Treading water should be a relaxed, efficient action of gently and slowly drawing your hands and forearms back and forth through the water. Your palms should be down in a sculling action out from the sides of the body, while your legs gently press in an alternating scissors kick or whip kick action. You should exert only the effort needed to maintain your face above the surface. No effort should be made to keep the entire head and shoulders up. The most important thing to remember is to RELAX. If you are required to stay afloat for an extended period of time, the survival floating method should be used.

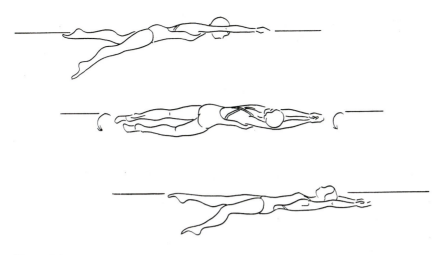

Figure 5.4
Turning over from prone to supine position.

Survival Floating

It is easy to learn a method of staying afloat and progressing through the water in conjunction with the modified breaststroke pull and bobbing technique that you learned in chapter 4.

You will find that you can relax and rest in very deep water for an indefinite period of time. It is particularly important to know this skill when you are boating, water skiing, or find yourself in deep water after an accident.

Begin practicing this skill in chest-deep water and later progress to deeper water.

First—Take a deep breath and assume a tuck float position (page 28). Relax and allow your arms and legs to dangle so that you can rest.

Second—Bring your arms up to your chest and stretch them forward along the surface, as you allow your legs to spread to a forward and back position similar to a wide step.

Third—Raise your head to "grab" a breath of air as your arms press around and down, and your legs squeeze together to support your body. Avoid bobbing high out of the water, but try to effortlessly raise your head only as high as necessary to inhale. Try to keep your chin on the water as you breathe in; exhale with your face in the water.

Fourth—Return to the tuck float with arms and legs dangling in a resting position. Repeat this four step pattern in a regular rhythm, breathing as normally as possible.

Do not thrust too hard on the upstroke of the press and kick, since the farther the head goes above the surface, the deeper you will sink underwater. Time your breathing by using the bobbing technique learned earlier to correspond to the up-and-down motion of your head. Lean slightly forward as you lift your head each time to facilitate your progress forward through the water.

Try to relax as much as possible. With practice, this technique can be continued for hours and may save your life if you find yourself in a position where you need to stay afloat for an extended period of time. For this reason it is called survival floating.

Why is it important in survival floating to **not** *thrust too hard on the upstroke of the press and kick?*

Standard Swimming Strokes

6

The seven standard swimming strokes are the elementary backstroke, the crawl, the back crawl, the sidestroke, the breaststroke, the inverted breaststroke, and the butterfly. Probably the easiest stroke to learn is the elementary backstroke.

The Elementary Backstroke

Stroke

The first stroke you should learn is the elementary backstroke (fig. 6.1). This is the most practical stroke for beginners because it takes so little effort and breathing is not a problem since the face remains out of the water throughout. Even a novice should be able to go great distances using this stroke without tiring.

The elementary backstroke is basically a three-beat rhythm stroke in which your arms and legs work almost simultaneously. Beginning from a supine glide position (fig. 6.1 a), the rhythm is (1) *recovery* of both arms and both legs (fig. 6.1 b, c), (2) *power* of both arms and both legs (fig. 6.1 d, e), and (3) *glide* with your body straight and relaxed, but controlled (fig. 6.1 f). This stroke is considered a resting stroke because of the long glide phase and the relatively effortless action involved. The key point to remember is that your body should be kept in a straight line without sagging or sitting, particularly during the recovery phase.

Whip Kick

Although there are several lateral moving kicks advocated by swimming instructors for use with the elementary backstroke, the most commonly used lateral kick is the whip kick. Most competitive swimmers use the whip kick in the racing breaststroke. The leg action of the whip kick is a recovery or power rhythm with a glide as follows: (1) from the back float position with legs extended, bend your knees, flex your ankles, rotate your toes outward, and spread your legs apart with as little hip drop as possible. (2) Pause slightly at this bent knee position, then extend and squeeze your legs together, while pointing your toes, for the press or power phase. The legs should be spread to about a forty-five degree angle as they are extended out and around. Hold your legs and

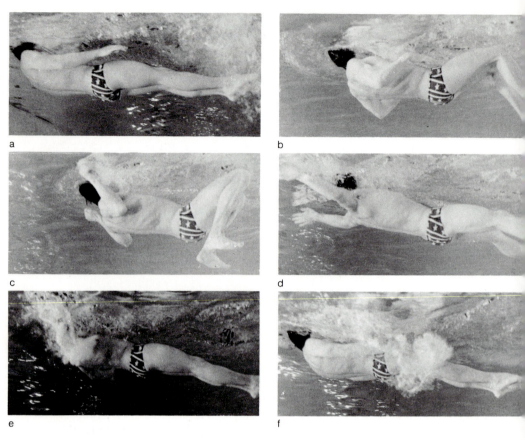

a   b

c   d

e   f

Figure 6.1
The elementary backstroke.

ankles fully extended during the glide until your momentum diminishes. Your thighs should neither be rotated in nor out during the entire cycle of the kick, but should be held with the kneecaps forward in relation to your body position.

Arm Stroke

The recovery of the arms is begun just prior to starting the leg recovery. Your hands should be drawn up your sides to your armpits, keeping your arms as close to the body as possible. Both arms are drawn up simultaneously with the elbows in. At this point, your wrists rotate so that the fingertips point out away from your shoulders. Knife your arms to full extension, fingertips first, out to the sides at an angle approximately shoulder height or slightly higher as the legs are being recovered. Shoulder-girdle flexibility and body control in the stroke will determine the height of the arm recovery. At this point both arms and both legs are fully extended to the sides to begin the power phase of the stroke. Pull your arms directly down to the sides just under the surface with elbows slightly bent so that the entire press is being exerted toward the feet as the legs are squeezed together. The inside of the feet and legs should be forcefully pressed against the water. Glide with both arms and both legs pressed close to the midline of your body in a "good posture" position.

At no point throughout the stroke should your arms or legs break the surface of the water. The rhythm should be regular and a long glide (about three seconds) should always be held. The most common errors are: (1) drawing your knees up out of the water rather than dropping your heels down; (2) bending at your hips, (which results in a sagging or sitting action) rather than keeping the body in good straight alignment; (3) breaking the *recovery, power, glide* rhythm by not starting your arm recovery sooner than your leg recovery (the power of both arms and both legs should not be exerted at the same time); and (4) not always starting and finishing each complete stroke with a glide (fig. 6.1f).

Why are these two actions considered to be errors in the elementary backstroke: starting the arm and leg recovery simultaneously and omitting a glide between strokes?

The Front Crawl Stroke

Stroke

The front crawl is the stroke best known by people in the United States. This stroke is referred to as "free-style" in competitive swimming and is presently the fastest stroke any person swims. There are several versions, but the "American crawl" is done with one complete arm stroke of both arms to six kicks. Your arms pull and recover alternately while your legs execute a continuous up-and-down flutter action. One arm starts the pull or power phase on kick "one" while the other arm is recovered, and the second arm starts the pull or power phase on kick "four" while the first arm is recovered. There is no glide phase to this stroke—some power is exerted throughout (fig. 6.2).

Flutter Kick

The flutter kick is used in the front crawl stroke with a six-beat leg kicking action. You should kick from the hip with your legs nearly straight and relaxed. Your knees should bend slightly with ankles extended throughout and toes pointed slightly in. Your kick should be an alternating up-and-down press in a deep (approximately eighteen inches), but fairly rapid rhythm (fig. 6.2). Keep your legs and feet underwater throughout the kick with no more than your heel breaking the surface at any time. (Review chapter 4 for flutter kick description.)

Arm Stroke

The arm stroke of the crawl is an alternating pull and recovery action with one arm pulling while the other is recovering. Your thumb should enter the water directly ahead of the shoulder (fig. 6.2 c). Fully extend your arm just under the water surface at entry to "catch" the water prior to the pull (fig. 6.2 d). Pull

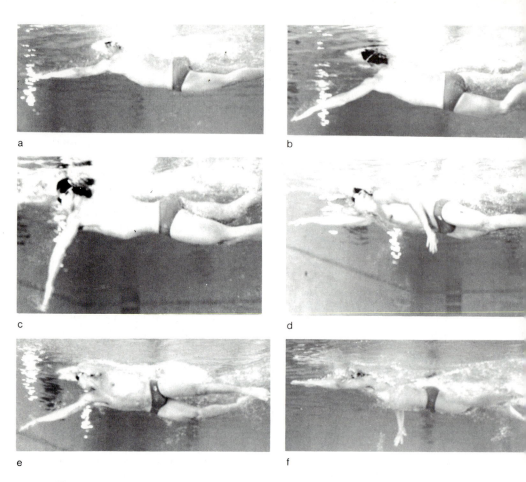

a b c d e f

Figure 6.2
The front crawl. (a) Left arm forward, right arm back, legs straight, head up to breathe.
(b) Left arm begins to come down, left leg begins to kick, head begins to come down.
(c) Left arm is down, right arm is up, head is in the water, legs are kicking. (d) Left arm
comes back, right arm straight ahead, head in the water. (e) Right arm comes down, left
arm comes up, head begins to come up. (f) Left arm is forward, right arm is down, head is
up for air.

your hand and forearm back, close to the midline of the body with your elbow
slightly bent (fig. 6.2 e), and then press on through the hip (fig. 6.2 f) causing
an in-out, pull-push action. This pull-push action should describe an hourglass-
shaped pull from in front of the shoulder, past the chest and through to the side
of the body, releasing at the hip. Power should be exerted throughout the entire
pull phase of each arm cycle.

The pull-push technique takes advantage of Newton's third law of motion:
For every action, there is an equal and opposite reaction. As you pull or push
the water toward your feet, the reaction drives your body forward. If you
pushed the water down toward the bottom of the pool, the reaction would tend

to raise your body out of the water rather than drive you forward. Therefore, stress a long pull which is parallel to the surface of the water while swimming, and draw your pull in an in-and-out pattern through to the hip.

Recover your arm over the water from the hip to the point of entry in front of the shoulder. Neither a tightly bent arm nor a stiff straight arm is desirable in the recovery. A relaxed, rounded arm position with your elbow held higher than your hand is preferred. As your first arm starts to pull, your second arm should be completing its pull and starting its recovery. Continuous pull and recovery action should be incorporated. Remember each phase by following these simplified steps: 1) entry 2) catch 3) pull 4) push 5) release and 6) recovery.

Why is it important in the front crawl stroke to start the pull with one arm just before, rather than after, the other arm completes its pull? Why is a straight arm pull inadvisable?

Breathing and Timing

To execute the total stroke, start as in a prone float and flutter kick with the water level at the hairline, your arms extended out in front, and your body straight. First the kick should be started, then the arm pull should be added and, finally, the breathing should begin. Take a breath of air by drawing in a short gasp as your head is turned to the side, just far enough to inhale through the mouth. Then turn your face back into the water and gradually exhale with a final spurt just prior to the next inhalation. Your face should be turned toward the pulling arm for the gulp of air just as the pull is being completed, and your face should be turned directly back into the water as that arm starts its recovery. Keep your body in good alignment throughout the stroke with no up-and-down motion or rolling action when your head is turned for the breath. Throughout the stroke, the hairline should be kept at the surface of the water, and the kick should be kept just under the surface.

Proper head position will result in a wave in front of your head and a trough next to your mouth. With practice, you can learn to catch a breath of air from the trough without actually raising your mouth above the level of the surrounding water. Many novice swimmers lift their head as they turn it for a breath and kick the feet above the surface of the water in the front crawl stroke. Ask a partner to check your stroke for these faults.

The Back Crawl

Stroke

The back crawl is racing's backstroke. This is the only competitive swimming stroke done other than in a prone position, and the truly all-around swimmer is always proficient in the backstroke. As in the front crawl, the back crawl is done with an alternating pull and recovery arm stroke and a continuous flutter kick. Your arms are recovered over the water and there should be one complete arm stroke (two arms) to six kicks with one arm pull starting on kick "one" and the second beginning on kick "four." The power of the kick is exerted on the "up" action and both your arms and legs are kept comfortably straight throughout the stroke. There should be no glide phase in this stroke as action is continuous.

Flutter Kick

To start the kick of the back crawl, use the same flutter action that was used in the front crawl and strongly emphasize the power or lift in the "up" action as in kicking a football. Keep your ankles extended throughout your kick with your toes turned slightly in toward the midline of the body. To gain maximum force from your kick, each leg must reach full extension on the up-and-down action of this six-beat kick. Your hips should be held high, your legs and feet should be kept under water throughout the kick, and mounds of water should be raised above the top of the foot on the lift of each leg. Your alternating up-and-down leg action should be deep but rapid and relaxed (fig. 6.3).

The back flutter kick is different from the front flutter kick in that on the downstroke the knees are straight, but on the upstroke, the knee is slightly bent then vigorously extended as the kick is completed. A hard lifting action with the top of the foot should be used.

Arm Stroke

The alternating pull and recovery action of the arm stroke is similar to that of the crawl stroke. Your little finger should enter the water first, almost directly above the shoulder (fig. 6.3 a). Knife your hand into the water to "catch" the water prior to the start of the pull (fig. 6.3 b). As your hand and forearm are pulled through, keep your elbow bent slightly to pull diagonally under the water (fig. 6.3 c). Give a final press at the hips on the last part of your arm stroke (fig. 6.3 d). This pull-push action creates a driving force all the way from above the shoulder through to your hip. Your arm is then recovered over the water, completely straight, from the hip to the entry position, with your wrist rotated on the recovery to permit your little finger to enter the water first. As one arm starts the pull, the other should be completing its pull and starting its recovery. The pull and recovery action should be continuous without a glide or stop at the side of the body. You can remember the six phases of the back crawl with the same six simplified cues that you used in the front crawl including: 1) entry 2) catch 3) pull 4) push 5) release and 6) recovery.

Timing

Start the back crawl stroke from a back float and flutter kick position with your arms extended overhead, both arms in the water as in the supine float and flutter kick. Add the kick, concentrating on keeping your body in good alignment, ears in the water and chin neither tucked way down nor lifted way up. From this point, pull one arm through to the hip to begin the arm cycle, and you are

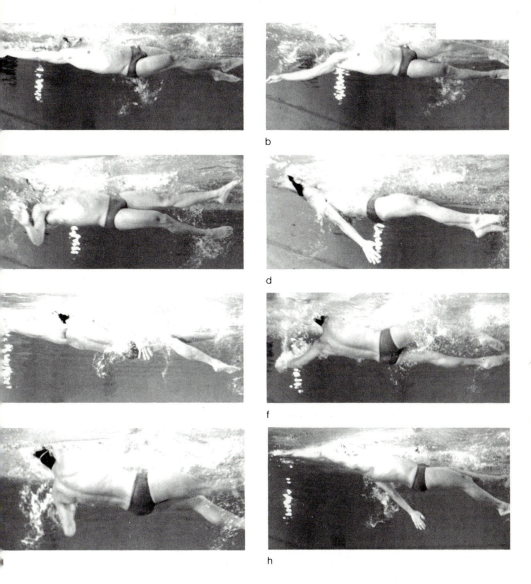

b

d

f

h

Figure 6.3
The back crawl. (a) Body straight, arms straight, legs kicking. (b) Legs kicking, right arm begins to come down, left arm begins to come up. (c) Legs kicking, right arm continues to come down as left goes up. (d) Right arm starts to come up. (e) Left arm straight out, right arm down. (f) Left arm continues to come down. (g) Legs kicking, left arm comes down. (h) Right arm straight out, left arm straight down.

on your way. Although breathing is not a problem since the face is maintained above water, it should be as rhythmic and natural as possible. Be sure that your arm is kept straight on the recovery and is not raised over your face or behind your head. The arm should be kept in a diagonal position above the water and enter above the shoulder. The body should be held in good alignment with no "sitting" or bending sideways. The body does however roll on its longitudinal axis with each arm stroke. When the right arm is reaching back, the body should be rolled slightly to the right with the right ear in contact with the upper part of the right shoulder. When the left arm reaches back, the roll is to the left. This rolling action allows for a greater reach of the arms and provides for a more powerful arm stroke (fig. 6.3).

The Sidestroke

Stroke

The sidestroke is not a competitive swimming stroke, but it is invaluable for lifesaving purposes. It is called the sidestroke because you lie on your side in the water with one arm and one leg on the top and the others on the bottom. The bottom arm is extended in the direction you are swimming and your head rests on that shoulder with your face turned slightly upwards and your body extended (fig. 6.4 a). The sidestroke is also one of the least tiring strokes since it has a glide phase and you are using the powerful muscles of your legs.

The sidestroke rhythm consists of a *pull* with the bottom or extended arm while the legs are preparing to kick and the top arm is preparing to push, then a *kick* as the legs press together and the top arm pushes toward the feet. The final action is to return the bottom arm to the extended position as your body is extended and *glide*. Complete the stroke by holding the glide position for about two seconds.

Scissors Kick

Work your sidestroke equally on both sides with no more practice on one side than on the other so that you can switch from one side to the other with confidence. This kick is often referred to as the "scissors" kick, for the legs make a scissoring action in exerting power. From the glide position, draw your legs up by bending both the knees and the hips until the hip and knee joints are at approximately ninety-degree angles (fig. 6.4 c, e). Extend your legs forward and back, rather than laterally, from the hip, with the top leg moving forward and the bottom leg moving back. Your forward ankle should be flexed in a toe-up position and your back ankle should be extended in a toe-pointed position (fig. 6.4 e). At this point, pause slightly to "grab" the water just prior to the press or power phase in which your legs are squeezed hard together to full leg and ankle extension (fig. 6.4 f). This is the most efficient kick to use in the survival floating technique described earlier, and is also the most valuable kick in lifesaving skills.

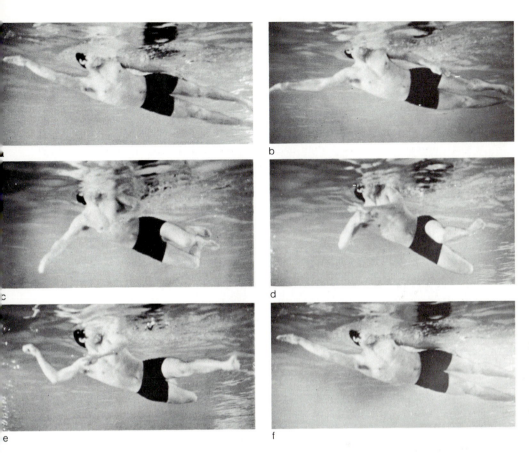

b

d

c

e   f

Figure 6.4
The sidestroke.

Two common errors in the scissors kick are separating the legs laterally and reaching forward with the lower leg. Have a partner check whether your performance is correct in these respects.

Arm Stroke

The arm pattern of the sidestroke is not particularly powerful but it is a stabilizing agent for the forceful thrust of the kick, as well as a support for the head. From the glide position, pull your lower extended arm diagonally under the upper body to the chest area with the elbow slightly bent and your fingertips pointing down so that the hand and forearm can be used to attain maximum power (fig. 6.4 b, c). At this point, bend your elbow tightly to your body (fig. 6.4 d) while your wrist is rotated to permit the fingertips to knife just under the surface of the water (fig. 6.4 e) in the recovery back to the glide position (fig. 6.4 f). As your bottom or extended arm starts the pull, the top arm is drawn up the side of your body (fig. 6.4 c) and then your fingertips stretch diagonally out in front of the chest to start the pull (fig. 6.4 d). The top arm push is a short hand and forearm, push or press from the chest area down to your hip (fig. 6.4 e, f). Your top arm and both legs are recovered while the lower arm pulls, and your lower arm is recovered as your top arm and legs exert power. Each complete stroke should be followed by a long glide phase.

Timing

The sidestroke, like any gliding or resting stroke, should be started and finished with a glide. Good body alignment is essential for maximum success with a minimum of effort. Your extended arm should be kept just under your head at the surface of the water until the pull is started, and your top arm and both legs should be held together until the recovery is started. Neither lift your head up out of the water nor drop it deep into the water, but keep your face turned up so that it is above the surface at all times. Since your face is out of the water, breathing is not a problem but it should be rhythmic and as normal as possible. Be very certain to work equally hard on each side in the sidestroke and be sure that your top leg always stretches forward (fig. 6.4).

The Breaststroke

Stroke

The breaststroke is done entirely in a prone position with a simultaneous pull of both arms followed by a simultaneous kick of both legs into a full body extension and glide. A competitive swimming stroke, the breaststroke has many and varied styles. One factor common to all, however, is parallelism. Both arms and both legs must work simultaneously and remain parallel to each other in relation to the surface throughout the stroke (fig. 6.5).

Arm Stroke

From an arms-extended prone glide position draw your hands and forearms diagonally back and down, with the elbows bending on the pull so the hands and forearms can be used as broad paddles. The pull is a short, whipping movement carried only to shoulder level with the elbows held high and fingertips held diagonally out and down (fig. 6.5 b, c). Whip your forearms in under the chin with a final thrust before your recovery and knife your fingertips close to the surface and through the water back to the extended position. Your elbows should remain wider than your hands at all times throughout the stroke (fig. 6.5 d, e).

Whip Kick

The kick is started with the recovery beginning just as your hands start to pull. Your knees should be bent to a ninety-degree angle or more as your legs are dropped at the hips with your knees bent and your ankles flexed and apart. Your knees should be together but pointing forward in relation to your body.

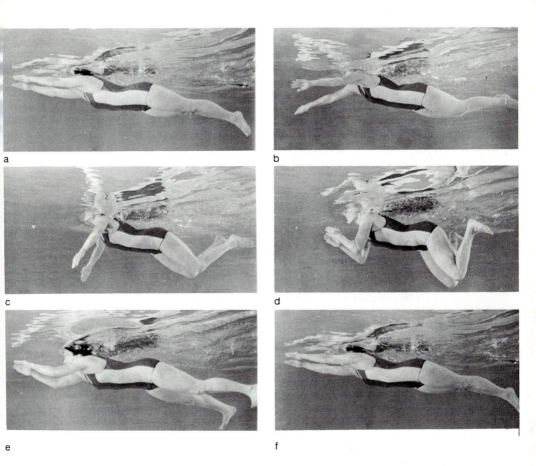

a b

c d

e f

Figure 6.5
The breaststroke.

Your heels should be wider than your knees and about shoulder distance apart (fig. 6.5 c, d). There is a slight hesitation at this point to "catch" the water prior to the press. On the kick, press your feet out and back in a circular, whipping action with the soles and insides of your feet and ankles feeling the greatest resistance (fig. 6.5 e, f). There should be a slight thigh rotation in the power phase. It is extremely important that your ankles be flexed on the recovery and extended *during* the kick in order to secure the maximum power. Finish your kick with a full leg extension into the glide (fig. 6.5 f).

Breathing and Timing

Breathing in the breaststroke is added in a *pull* and *inhale, kick, glide* rhythm. Your head should be raised very slightly as the arms start the pull in order to take a shorter breath of air; then drop your head immediately back into the water and exhale as the power phase of the kick is being exerted. A final thrust of air should be blown out just prior to a new breathing cycle.

Start the breaststroke from a prone float position with your face in the water. As the arm pull is started, stretch your chin forward on the water as you raise your head to breathe. Draw your legs up with feet flexed and apart; pause prior to the press. As your arms are extended forward into the recovery, press your legs and feet out and down to a fully extended position. Finish your stroke in a full prone glide. You can remind yourself of your stroke rhythm by using these cues: 1) reach 2) pull 3) kick and recovery 4) reach (fig. 6.5).

The Inverted Breaststroke

Stroke

The inverted breaststroke is probably the most difficult stroke for the average swimmer. It starts in the supine glide position, with the arms stretched overhead. From the arms-extended glide position, pull your arms down to your hips, and as your arms recover, draw your legs up to press out and around in the whip kick. The leg press is taken as the arms are stretched overhead in the recovery. Finish the stroke in an arms-overhead supine glide position.

A common problem in the breaststroke and in the inverted breaststroke is failure to make the action of the legs symmetrical throughout the entire kick. Ask a partner to check this carefully for you. This error would disqualify you in competition.

Arm Stroke

The arm pull differs from other strokes in that the pull is taken from the full arm extension overhead to the hips, effecting a pull all the way to the hips (fig. 6.6 a–d). The arms are recovered from the hips to approximately the shoulders before the recovery of the kick is completed (fig. 6.6 f). In this part of the recovery your arms should be kept as close to the body as possible. Your arms are then stretched overhead as the power of the kick is exerted. Complete your stroke in an arms-overhead glide.

Whip Kick

The kick of the inverted breaststroke is the same as the kick used in the elementary backstroke. Your lower legs are dropped with heels apart, feet flexed, and knees together, but pointing forward in relation to your body (fig. 6.6 e–g). From this recovery, your feet are pressed out and around with the bottom and insides of your feet feeling the greatest pressure. Be sure the whip action is out and around, all in one motion (fig. 6.6 g, h). Glide with your feet together and your legs straight (fig. 6.6 i).

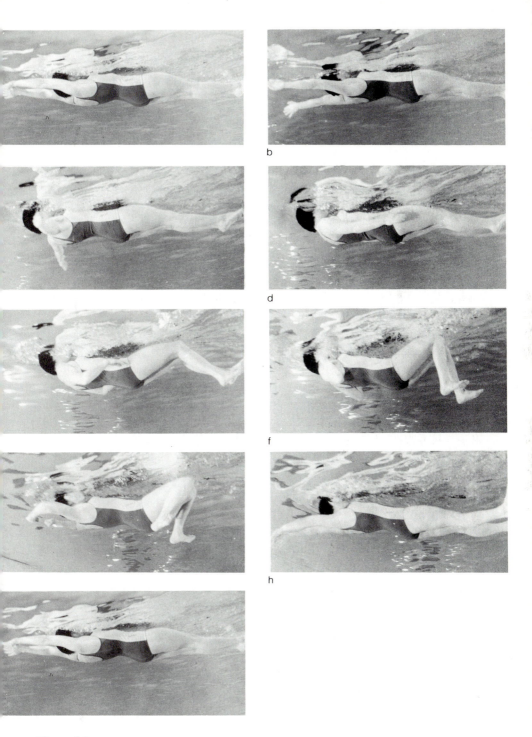

b

d

f

h

Figure 6.6
The inverted breaststroke.

Breathing and Timing

Breathing should not be a problem, for again the face should be above the surface at all times. The most effective breathing action is an inhalation on the pull and an exhalation on the kick. A slight alternate tucking and dropping back of the head adds to the efficiency and fluidity of the stroke. As the pull is taken, bring your head slightly forward into a chin tucked position and as the whip of your kick is exerted, drop your head slightly back into a chin-up position as you stretch into the glide.

The timing of the inverted breaststroke is not difficult if you think of starting and finishing each stroke in a glide position with arms overhead. You may have some trouble keeping the face above the surface at first, a difficulty which is usually a result of either drawing your knees up too high on the recovery of your kick or ''sitting'' in the water, but smoothing out the other parts of the stroke will help you correct these faults. Use the same cues in this stroke as you used in the breaststroke: 1) reach 2) pull 3) kick and recovery 4) reach (fig. 6.6).

The Butterfly Stroke

Stroke

This stroke is used in all aspects of swimming competition. The butterfly has become the second fastest stroke known, but because of its extreme difficulty, it is rarely perfected by noncompetitive swimmers. Because it is the most exhausting form of swimming, one must be in excellent condition to perform the butterfly stroke for any length of time. The butterfly is done by pulling both arms, simultaneously and parallel to each other, from an extended position overhead through to the hips. The arms are then recovered over the water, simultaneously and parallel to each other, back to the extended position. A double leg kick is accented at the start and again at the completion of each arm pull (fig. 6.7).

Dolphin Kick

The most common rhythm of the butterfly stroke is two kicks to one complete arm stroke. There is a major kick as the arm pull is started and a minor kick as the arm recovery is started. Actually the power of the two kicks would be the same except that the force needed to lift the arms over the water causes one kick to press deeper, thus giving an appearance of an alternation between a major and a minor kicking action. Your kick should be a full-body press from a pike to an arch at the hips followed by a continuous up-and-down press of the knees, ankles, and feet. It is important, however, to avoid dropping the hips as you execute this kick since that action results in an inefficient up and down motion and too much bend in the knees. If you have difficulty in recovering

Figure 6.7
The butterfly stroke. (a) Hips up, chest and head down, arms above head, parallel with body. (b) Head up, arms down, body is straight. (c) Arms straight to side, knees bent, feet up, head up, body straight. (d) Head down, arms up, knees bent, feet coming down. (e) Head up, body straight, feet down. (f) Arms over head, chest and feet down, hips up.

your arms over the water, you are probably dropping your hips too much. The legs and feet must be parallel to each other throughout the kick. The legs must move simultaneously and equal power should be exerted both up and down in each kick.

Arm Stroke

The arm stroke is a double arm pull and over-the-water recovery with simultaneous arm action throughout. Your hands should knife into the water, thumbs first, in front of the shoulders with your elbows held higher than your hands. Both hands and forearms are then pulled back, with elbows high, in an out-in-out hourglass-shaped pattern to just under the hips. This *pull-push* action effects a stronger power phase in your arm stroke. Recover your arms simultaneously over the water to knife again into the entry, thumbs first to keep your elbows high as you reach into the water in front of your shoulders. There is no glide taken in this stroke as the arm action is continuous.

Breathing and Timing

Breathing in the butterfly stroke is, and must be, a conscious effort in order to maintain the consistent stroke rhythm. Often your head is raised too soon or too late which causes an up-and-down motion in the stroke rather than a smooth, gliding forward motion. Just as in the breaststroke, your chin should be stretched forward at the surface and your head lifted slightly. Inhale as your arm pull is started, and drop your head back into the water as the back press of the arm stroke is taken. Exhale under water with a final out thrust just prior to the next breath. Your head may be lifted directly forward or to the side for breathing provided your shoulders are held squarely parallel to the surface.

Counting a kick on the downbeat, the total rhythm of the butterfly stroke is a *pull-kick-kick*. It is a down kick of the legs at the end of the first "pulling" part of the arm stroke and a second down kick of the legs on the final "pressing" arm action out of the water to the recovery. You might think of this kick sequence as you start the pull and again as you start the recovery (fig. 6.7).

Turns at the Pool Wall

Most swimming instruction takes place in pools, so beginners should learn to make a quick and efficient turn at the wall. Since both hands contact the wall simultaneously in the breaststroke, you can simply pull your feet and knees up under your body and put your feet on the wall about two feet below the surface. Then, as you drop under water, release one hand in the direction of your turn, push off, and roll into a prone position as you stretch into a glide. Hold the glide until your momentum slows down, then begin the stroke again. This is sometimes called a "grab" turn and is also used in the butterfly stroke (fig. 6.8).

The same turn may be used in the crawl, but only one hand makes contact with the wall. Your feet hit the wall already having turned about ninety degrees so that one is above the other and they are pointed sideways. You then push off as hard as possible and complete the other ninety degrees of the turn around the long axis as you stretch into the glide. Again, glide for a few seconds, then resume stroking. A more advanced turn for the front crawl, called the "flip turn" is described later.

The back crawl turn also uses a one-hand grab on the wall, but your legs tuck up in front of you and you turn sideways so that your back always stays toward the bottom of the pool. As your feet swing around and contact the wall, you should still be holding on with one hand. The push off is then straight

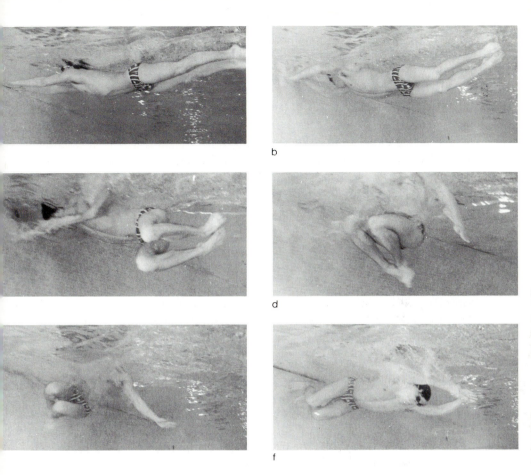

b

d

f

Figure 6.8
The "grab" turn is used in both the breaststroke and the butterfly stroke.

backward into a back glide and stroke. If your right arm hits the wall first, tuck your legs and turn to the right. The opposite is true if the left hand hits first (fig. 6.9).

In a free-style sprint race, a quick turn at the wall is required to start the next lap. Good swimmers execute a somersault or "flip" turn in order to lose a minimum amount of time at the wall. This technique starts by diving one arm down into the water as you approach the end of the pool. As your head is tucked, flip your legs over the water in a somersaulting action and place your feet firmly on the wall. Push off the wall on your side and roll to a prone glide position with your arms stretched overhead. Hold this glide position to take advantage of the strong push of the legs, kick to the surface, and then resume stroking (fig. 6.10).

Can you describe the leg action for the front crawl and breaststroke "grab" turns? Can you describe the "flip" turn and the turn for the back crawl?

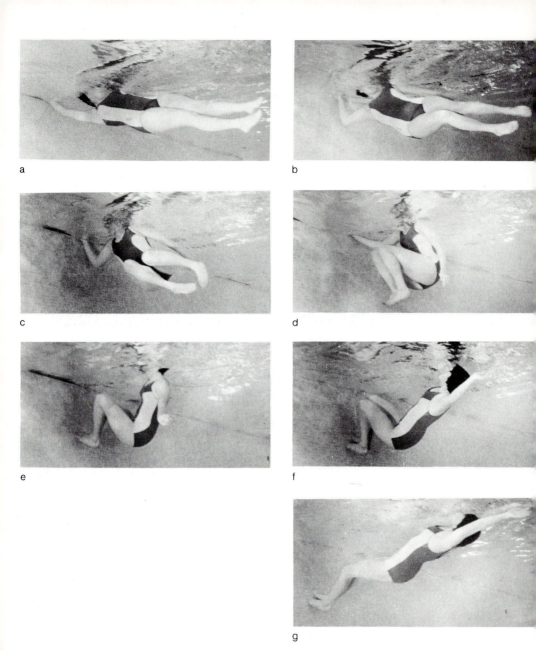

a

b

c

d

e

f

g

Figure 6.9
Back crawl turn.

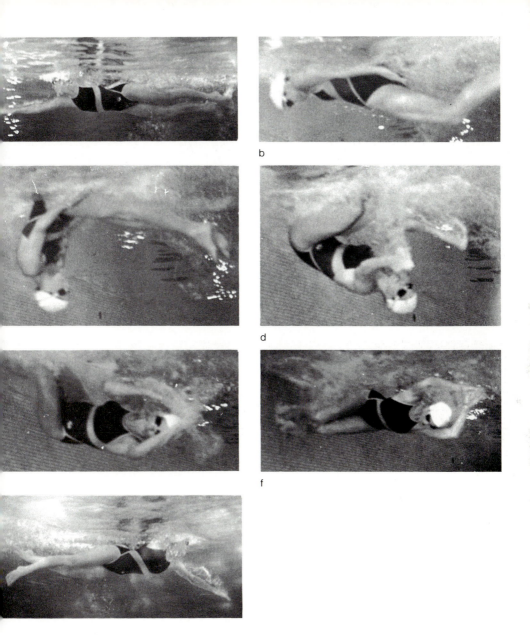

Figure 6.10

Flip turn. (a) Body straight, left arm up, right arm straight forward. (b) Arms back, head tucked to chest, knees bent. (c) Legs straight, head down, to form "L" with body. (d) Head comes down farther to form a straight-legged somersault. (e) Feet are up to push off, knees bent, body begins to twist. (f) Knees and feet come down, arms are over the head completing twist. (g) Twist is completed, legs and body straight to begin stroke.

Beginning Diving

7

Jumping and Diving

It is extremely important that you know the conditions of the water before you enter. You should never jump into a pool or lake without first knowing the depth, the temperature, and whether or not there is anyone swimming there. A weak swimmer in particular should check the depth. Many times a novice is caught in water just slightly over his or her head as a result of poor judgment. You should note the depth in order to avoid injury from a too shallow entry. Note the temperature of the water to avoid shock, muscle cramp, or tenseness from fear and cold. All swimmers should avoid careless entry into unknown or dark water or water that is too shallow for jumping or diving. Often the skilled swimmer is prone to horseplay, and injuries can result from jumping or diving on other swimmers.

Jumping and Leveling Off

You must learn how to jump into the water, level the body off, and proceed into a stroke before you can safely swim in deep water. This skill should be practiced until you can jump into water well over your head and surface into a stroke with ease. Before jumping, make sure the area is clear of other swimmers. To jump, step clear of the deck and keep your feet under your body. Spread your legs into a scissors kick and keep your arms out to the sides to keep your body from going too deep into the water. In the water, tuck your body with chin in and knees to your chest, then extend your legs back and your arms forward to a prone float and flutter kick position. Flutter kick to the surface and swim away (fig. 7.1).

Deck Diving

From the jump into the water you should progress to a stationary dive into deep water. If you are a beginner, you should first kneel on the side of the pool. With the toes of one foot curled over the edge and your head down, extend your arms out and down from the shoulders so that your arms are over your ears. This may also be practiced from water level by sitting on the deck with both feet on the pool gutter (fig. 7.2). From this position, allow yourself to roll forward, reaching for the bottom of the pool with your fingertips. The most important thing is to keep your arms over your ears and to reach for the bottom of the pool. Do not lift your head to look where you are diving, but lead with

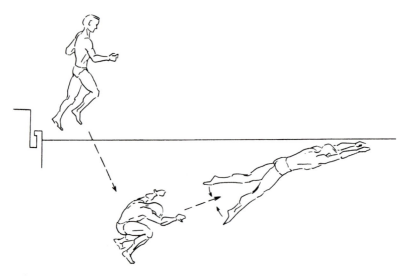

Figure 7.1
Entering deep water and leveling off.

the top of your head. This will cause you to go several feet under the water, so be sure the depth is sufficient (at least seven or eight feet). When you are under water, arch your back, raise your head and arms toward the surface, and flutter kick up.

Once the kneeling dive is accomplished, advance to a standing position. Again, with toes curled over the side, bend down with your arms stretched over your ears, as before. Bend down far enough so that the fingertips are pointing toward the bottom of the pool and not out away from you. Keeping arms straight, legs straight, and head down, allow your body to roll forward to enter headfirst, with fingertips reaching for the bottom of the pool. As skill increases, start standing straighter and bending at the waist as the body is rolled forward to enter the water, fingertips first. Later, a spring may be added to complete the dive from the side of the pool (fig. 7.2).

Diving from a Board

Stationary Diving

The use of a springboard is an entirely different action than diving off a solid surface. Springboard diving should be approached with caution to avoid serious injury. As a first step, take the dive from a standing position, as was done from the side of the pool. Because of the additional height above the water, you should tuck your chin very slightly and aim farther out, but still reach toward the bottom of the pool with the fingertips. Once you have accomplished the standing dive, a gentle spring may be added. Again, you should be careful not to sharply tuck the chin on the takeoff for this will cause your body to flip over

Figure 7.2
Deck diving.

or your legs to slap your back. Continue diving from a standing position with a minimum spring until control is developed. You should be sure to hold your legs together and straight once you have taken off into the dive, and your arms should be straight and squeezed tightly over the ears on the entry into the water.

The Forward Approach and Hurdle

Once you have learned to control your body in standing dives, you must learn an "approach" before you can advance to the more difficult categories. A legal approach in international competitive diving must have a minimum of four steps. These four steps should be made up of three walking steps and a jump which is called a "hurdle." You may take more steps if you wish, but no less than four. For maximum control, the approach steps should be taken slowly and deliberately. The hurdle should be equal in length to the preliminary steps and should lift the body up rather than forward or backward on the board. The take-off should be an elevating movement, again, *up* rather than *out* off the board. The arms should be controlled throughout the approach and takeoff, as well as in the dive itself. As the knee is lifted on the hurdle, raise both arms, then press to "ride the board" as you jump. Lift your arms again to raise the body forward and up off the board for the takeoff into a dive (fig. 7.3).

The Forward Dive in Pike Position

The first dive you should learn is the forward dive in pike position, which is better known as the "jackknife." With this dive you will learn to develop body control to become aware of your position. It is very important to avoid grabbing for the toes or tucking the chin, for these actions will throw the body well beyond center and cause a flipping action. Try instead to lift your hips above your shoulders into the pike position. Draw your feet up and forward toward the fingertips rather than your fingertips down to your feet; then look and reach for the bottom of the pool. A final stretch into the water completes the dive.

Figure 7.3
Springboard diving—the forward approach.

Progressing on to other dives is a matter of specific practice, but all dives are successful primarily because of the control and perfection of the approach and the use of the head in the dive.

Before diving for the first time from a springboard, you should mentally rehearse the actions of a dive from the deck while making two slight adjustments because of the board height. Do you know what these adjustments are?

The Back Dive

The back dive is relatively easy to perform off the low (one meter) board, but it usually frightens beginners because they cannot see where they are going. First try the back dive without a jump. Stand on the end of the board, facing the board, with your feet about halfway off the end of the board. Stretch your arms over your head and grasp one thumb with the other hand. This keeps the arms together and resists the force of the water on contact.

With your arms extended, squeeze your ears with your upper arms and keep your elbows straight. Do not bend your knees, rather arch your head and shoulders back to look and reach for the water. Let yourself fall back while looking and reaching for the water until you enter the water headfirst. Do not arch your lower back as you fall.

Failure to keep the head and shoulders back will result in a "back flop." A big arch in the small of the back or bent knees will cause you to arch too far over onto your stomach into the water. Successfully performing the above described action however, will guarantee a headfirst dive. Never practice a back dive from the side of the pool as too much arch will carry you into the pool wall and you may hit your head under water.

Figure 7.4
The back dive.

After the falling dive is mastered, a jump may be added. Begin by adding a small jump with limited arm action and progress to a full back dive action. Raise your arms to the sides and down, pressing the board downward with the legs and feet on the downward arm action. Extend your legs into a jump as you lift your arms overhead. At the top of your lift, lay your head and shoulders back to "set" your arms out to the sides, keeping the rest of your back and your legs straight. Look and reach for the water as you did in the standing dive, extending your arms overhead, close to your ears until your entire body is in the water. Stretch to the bottom of the pool (fig. 7.4).

Advanced Techniques

The key to learning more advanced techniques is to be flexible and well-rounded in your approach. Some of these techniques are learned for competitive purposes, some for symmetrical body development, some for eventual participation in such activities as lifesaving, synchronized swimming, speed swimming, scuba diving and water polo, and some are learned just for the fun of finding out how much you can do.

What should you note before jumping or diving into any body of water?

Surface Diving

Tuck Surface Dive

Getting under water from a position on the surface of the water is a skill that should be mastered by all participants in water sports. This ability is essential for lifesaving, scuba diving, and synchronized swimming and is a major part of any general swimming program. The simplest of the surface dives is the *tuck* surface dive. In this surface dive, your legs are tucked up from a prone glide position with your head held in line with the body. As the arms are pulled back to the hips and then down through the water toward the face, the chin is tucked. This action will cause your tucked body to roll forward into a dive. As your arms are almost in line with your face, extend your body so that your legs are stretched toward the sky. The lift of the legs will force your body down toward the bottom of the pool. You should avoid pulling too hard in the tuck position, or the head will pass the vertical line and the surface dive will take a sharp angle in under your body rather than straight down.

Pike Surface Dive

The next type of surface dive you should try is done in essentially the same way, but you keep your legs straight with the body in a *pike* position. The pike surface dive is started again from the prone glide position. From the prone glide, tuck the chin and pull your arms back to your hips. Then rotate your wrists in order to pull down in a circular motion toward the face. The body should be piked with the head in line with the body as the arms pull back. The legs should be lifted vertically as the arms are drawn from the hip level to the face. It is important that you make the one circular arm pull do the work and avoid tucking the chin to start down. A tuck of the chin will create the same error of diving as in the tuck surface dive and will cause you to dive at an angle rather than straight down (fig. 7.5).

Feetfirst and Swim-Down Surface Dives

There are two less common surface dives called the *feetfirst* and the *swim-down* surface dives. The feetfirst surface dive is used in unknown or dark water where the bottom may be hazardous. The swim-down surface dive is used for very shallow or fast-moving dives, such as are often needed in lifesaving. The feetfirst surface dive is started from a vertical position in deep water. Thrust your body out of the water by exerting a strong scissors or breaststroke kick. As your body starts down after the thrust, start your arm pull. Knife your arms down by the sides to the hips and then press up toward the surface in a

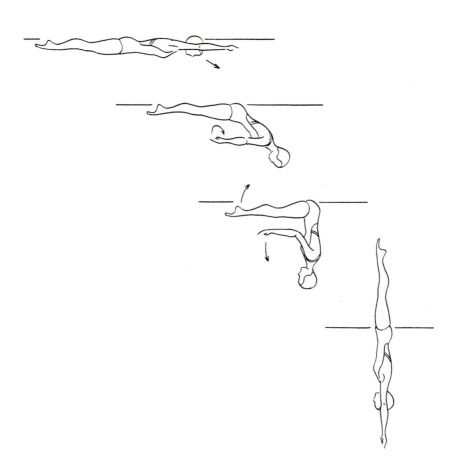

Figure 7.5
The pike surface dive.

palms-up pull, forcing the body to dive in a straight line, feetfirst toward the bottom of the pool. In this dive it is important to keep the body straight and in good alignment.

The swim-down surface dive is a simple tuck of the chin from a crawl or any other prone position which causes your body to start to drop. As your chin is tucked, both arms should be drawn back to the hips as in the tuck and pike surface dives. This action effects a shallow body dive, but there is no subsequent lift of the legs, only a hip bend. Consequently the depth that is achieved in the other dives is not accomplished here.

Under what circumstances should your choice of surface dive be the feetfirst dive? Can you give reasons for using the swim-down surface dive?

Special Water Activities

8

Swimming is fun. There are interesting and exciting things to do in the water regardless of your level of skill provided you practice safety skills and know your own abilities and strength limitations. Drownings usually occur as a result of unwise decisions or an overestimation of ability. After you have accurately evaluated your swimming skill, select those activities suited to your interest and personality.

Kinds of Activities

All ages enjoy flotation devices for leisurely or spirited play around a home pool. Anything from an old inner tube to a Styrofoam kickboard or tub is adequate support for water tag, races, or contests. Beach balls are great fun to dodge, pass, or shoot for corners or goals while the opposing team defends them. Diving for pennies, stones, or rubber bricks is also fun, but be careful when playing in a crowded pool and never leave trinkets sitting on the bottom when you are finished. Each pool situation will govern the rules of play.

Aqua Fitness

From pool jogging to formal aqua-aerobics classes, hundreds of people enjoy water exercises to control weight, strengthen and improve muscle tone and to keep their cardiovascular systems in good shape. Exercising in chest-deep water burns about twelve calories per minute and the continual resistance of the water is good exercise without muscular strain. Since your body weighs only ten percent of its real weight in the water, your muscles and joints will not experience the soreness or stress often felt in jogging or in doing aerobics in a gymnasium.

Some of the fitness activities enjoyed in pools include pool walking or jogging. Twenty to thirty minutes, three to four times a week of these activities can improve both muscle tone and cardiovascular fitness when you exaggerate your strides, maintain good posture and use your arms in a strong punching motion. Remember to use your entire foot, heel to toes, and keep your head erect. Doing lunges, walking backwards and sidewards, and variations of steps, kicks, jumps, and dance movements enhance the pleasure of water walking.

More formalized exercise programs are enjoyed by many in the form of aqua-aerobics. Generally, these programs use music to accompany the exercise routine. These programs vary from highly monitored classes that scientifically calculate blood pressure and heart rate and establish levels of conditioning and target training zones, to an unstructured neighborhood social group. To participate in fitness programs in the water it is advisable to have a physician's approval and to establish your program under the guidance of an instructor who is certified in aqua-aerobics. The rewards of a regular aqua-aerobics program, which can result in good health, cardiovascular fitness, and stress free muscular toning, are immeasurable!

Beach Swimming

Another type of water activity is found at the beach. While a wide variety of games are available there, one must *learn* to have fun at the beach. Many people avoid swimming at the beach because "the waves are too rough" when actually they just don't know how to enjoy them. When first learning about ocean or lake swimming, you should start slowly in waist-deep water. Try to jump gentle waves while turning to "give with the waves" rather than standing fast and resisting them. After the feeling of "giving" with the wave is established, try diving in under the wave. Just before the wave breaks, take a shallow dive right into it. Start by diving through light waves, for a stronger wave may tumble you over. Even a strong swimmer should be aware of danger signals and restricted areas at beaches. When storm warnings, undertow, or other restrictions are posted, *observe them!*

In addition to wave jumping or wave diving at the beach, it is fun to glide with the surf. Body surfing requires only a small wave. Beginning body surfers may choose to use a Styrofoam floatboard to help them along, but *air-filled* floatation devices should be used with caution at a beach. Board surfing is a great sport, and it has become so popular in some places that special surfing sites have been established where swimming is not permitted. Though there are different types of surfing, the essential goal is the same. The surfer must try to "catch" a wave by swimming hard just as it approaches and then, by either stretching his or her body or lying flat on the board, "ride" the wave into the shore. Board surfers can later learn to do many kinds of exciting moves and tricks on their boards.

Competitive Swimming and Diving

Other water activities include many varieties of sports and games. The racing enthusiast may choose to enter competitive swimming through the local Amateur Athletic Union (AAU), swim school, YMCA, YWCA, or club. In competitive swimming you may enter any of several events. The strokes included are the butterfly, the backstroke, the breaststroke, and free-style. Competitive swimming does not incorporate any of the other strokes. One may choose to swim any or all of these strokes in either sprints (short races) or distance (long races). Or become an all-around swimmer and compete in the individual medley—a race in which each swimmer performs each of the four strokes.

The person who is interested in form and control rather than speed may choose to participate in springboard diving, or synchronized swimming. In each, the body must be held in good form and controlled throughout the execution of a stroke, a figure, or a dive in order to win an event. Each of these activities is judged by a panel of experts and the diver, or synchronized swimmer, is awarded points according to the dive, stroke, or technical difficulty, and the perfection of execution. After each of the participants has performed the required number of dives, strokes, or techniques to the best of his or her ability, a winner is determined based on the maximum total of scores given multiplied by the point difficulty.

Skin and Scuba Diving

If you are a natural adventurer, you are probably interested in either skin or scuba (self-contained underwater breathing apparatus) diving. Both skin and scuba diving should be learned in a pool rather than in a lake or an ocean and you should never attempt scuba diving without expert instruction. The equipment needed in skin diving includes a mask, flippers, and a snorkel. In skin diving, your capacity to stay under water limits the extent to which you can explore the bottom of the swimming area. A real sports person however, enjoys the challenge of outwitting a fish with natural breath control. Others prefer skin diving for underwater exploration because scuba diving can be very dangerous unless you know appropriate air and underwater time calculations. Also the equipment (required in skin diving) is less expensive and less cumbersome than scuba gear.

In scuba diving, the swimmer is assisted in the ability to stay under water by a diving tank strapped to the back. If deep or cold water scuba diving is done, "wet suits" are also usually worn. Neither of these activities, particularly scuba diving, should be entered into lightly or with limited instruction. Knowledge and experience are essential to safety in the use of diving equipment, and instruction in the diving area, its currents, depths, and living creatures should be well established before a novice diver enters the water. If caution and understanding are assured, both skin and scuba diving are exciting and exhilarating activities.

Water Polo

The team-oriented sportsperson will most certainly enjoy the sport of water polo, but only a very strong swimmer can endure the rigors of this game. Since water polo is normally played in deep water, and the rules require a player to have his or her feet off the bottom of the pool while playing the ball, participation in this sport is strenuous exercise. Only modified versions of this game can be played in home pools, for the required depth and size are not common to them, and the official goals are cumbersome and require fittings in the pool deck. But whether it is played as a home version or as a competitive team sport, it is fun to develop the skills of passing the ball without touching the bottom and of scoring by getting the ball into a goal defended by your opponents.

Other water sports and games which require a knowledge of swimming are both fun and beneficial. Some of these are water skiing, boating, canoeing, sailing, and aquaplaning, but none of these water sports or games should be taken lightly. Knowledge and ability in basic swimming skills and the use of protective devices such as life jackets are a must to insure maximum safety, and only an experienced person should handle the boat or canoe.

Swimming, water games, and water sports are fun, healthful, and exhilarating if entered into wisely. The greater your understanding of all aspects of water skills, the greater potential you have for fun. Develop your skill and understanding of swimming and the water for maximum safety and enjoyment.

Other popular water activities include aqua-aerobics, inner-tube water polo, triatholon, long distance and therapeutic swimming. Participation in water activities such as these is not only fun and exhilarating but contributes to both strength and aerobic conditioning.

Of the many aquatic sports involving personal equipment, which requires the most exacting training in use and safety procedures?

Conditioning

9

Swimming is a fine sport to improve fitness since both muscular and cardio-respiratory endurance may be developed by participating in this activity. Competitive swimmers, scuba divers, synchronized swimmers, and lifeguards work out many hours each day to attain or maintain a desired level of performance.

If you are interested in becoming a competitive speed or synchronized swimmer, you should find a coach and work on your skill and stroke specialties as directed.

To improve your physical fitness through swimming, keep these things in mind:

1. Work out regularly and frequently (at least two or three times a week).
2. Use a variety of strokes with as many different kinds of kicks as possible.
3. Press yourself to do just a little more than you think you can. It will also help to work out with a friend or classmate of similar skill who can provide encouragement and competition. Swimming laps alone is dangerous and can also be boring.

Following are several ideas for workout patterns that you can use as guidelines in developing your daily program.

Nonswimmer (To be done at the shallow end of the pool.)

    4 × 1 width   Prone float and flutter kick with ten second back float to rest, repeat.

    4 × 1 width   Supine float and flutter bob ten times, repeat.

    4 × 1 width   Prone float and kick, roll to back to breathe, roll to face and continue.

Novice (To be done at the shallow end of the pool.)

    4 × 1 width   Elementary backstroke, turn and repeat.

    4 × 1 width   Prone float and flutter kick with ten second rest, repeat.

    4 × 1 width   Supine finning and flutter kick with ten second rest, repeat.

    4 × 1 width   Front crawl with ten second rest, repeat.

Beginner

2 × 25 yds	Front crawl with ten second rest, repeat.
4 × 25 yds	Elementary backstroke, no rest, repeat.
2 × 25 yds	Front crawl with ten second rest, repeat.
4 × 25 yds	Sidestroke (two each side), no rest, repeat.
2 × 25 yds	Back crawl with ten second rest, repeat.

(Stress *rest* on the glide during the resting strokes.)

Intermediate

4 × 75 yds	Two front crawl with one elementary backstroke, no rest.
3 × 75 yds	Two back crawl with one sidestroke, no rest.
3 × 75 yds	Two back crawl with one backstroke kick only, no rest.
3 × 75 yds	Two front crawl kick only with backstroke pull only, no rest.
4 × 75 yds	Two front crawl with one backstroke, no rest.

Advanced

4 × 100 yds	Kick only with ten second rest, repeat.
4 × 100 yds	Pull only with ten second rest, repeat.
4 × 100 yds	Free-style with twenty second rest, repeat.
4 × 100 yds	Stroke specialty and regular distance—swim—rest.
2 × 100 yds	Stroke weakness with twenty seconds rest.
4 × 100 yds	Free-style or 16 × 25 yards free-style, maximum speed.
4 × 100 yds	Kick only easy speed.

These workouts are recommendations, merely ideas from which your specific program may be developed. Workouts should be designed for each individual based on his or her skill, physical condition, and desired goals. In planning a workout you should: 1) vary your strokes and alternate rest phases, 2) do not rest as long as it takes to recover normal breathing, and 3) force yourself to swim as fast as you can while maintaining good stroke form. As your skill and efficiency improve, the work phase should be increased and the rest phase decreased. This advanced workout totals a mere 2600 yards. A typical workout of serious competitive swimmers often totals 6000 or more yards.

Workouts can only be as effective as the output of the swimmer. To improve your physical skill and condition, you must make demands on your body by "pressing" in the workout. The harder you work, the faster you will improve, but even a lazy, or light workout is better than none.

As you master the techniques of various strokes and dives, you should also work to increase your endurance. Can you now tread water for two minutes? Four minutes? Six minutes? Can you swim 440 yards in under twelve minutes? Ten minutes? Eight minutes?

Competitive Swimming and Diving

10

By the time you have mastered most of the strokes and techniques described in this work, you may have developed a desire to enter competitive swimming or diving. Since this book is designed for beginners and intermediates, only some of the skills that are necessary for competition are introduced here. For more information, you may refer to any of several excellent books on pages 79–80. They discuss in great detail competitive styles, workout schedules, and coaching techniques.

Competitive Swimming

In competitive swimming, only four strokes are used; the free-style, the backstroke, the breaststroke, and the butterfly. In the free-style race, the participants may swim any stroke, except one of the other competitive strokes. Since the crawl is the fastest stroke it is used almost exclusively in the free-style event. For the sprints, which are 50, 100, or 200 yards or meters long, most freestylers modify their breathing so that they do not breathe after each arm cycle. Usually they will take several cycles of the arms between each breath, and in the short races, they may swim a whole length without breathing. Because this change in technique presents less drag in the water and does not interrupt stroke rhythm as much, the swimmer can usually cover short distances faster. Except for this change, the competitive free-style is the same as the crawl stroke explained in chapter 6.

During longer distances such as the 400 and 1500 meter races, most freestylers breathe every one or two arm cycles. In these races which last longer, the body cannot tolerate lack of oxygen without reducing work output. Consequently, distance swimmers have to breathe more often than sprinters.

All races, except the backstroke, start with a racing dive from a block which is no higher than thirty inches off the water. You should push off the starting block angled slightly up then pike down into the water. You should dolphin your legs to bring your upper body back to the surface (fig. 10.1).

Backstrokers start the race in the water with their feet on the wall or gutter and their hands on the gutter or starting block. You should dive up and back off the block. Thrust your arms around to the sides and overhead as the gun sounds then glide on your back taking full advantage of the thrust of the start before starting the kick and then the arm stroke.

a

b

c

Figure 10.1
The racing start.

The competitive backstroke is the backstroke described in chapter 6. The backstroke turn presents a special problem since the rules require that the swimmer touch and leave the wall on his or her back. To execute this turn, swim into the wall, drop your head back, and reach the extended arm down the wall to touch about eighteen inches under water. Lift your legs up and over the water, pivoting on the shoulder of the extended arm in a side somersault, firmly "planting" your feet on the wall. Extend your arms overhead as you push off into a supine glide, kick to the surface, and resume stroking.

The competitive breaststroke is somewhat different from the conventional breaststroke. In competition, the glide is eliminated and you should kick as soon as your arms start to extend forward after completion of your stroke. Breathing is done more quickly and consists of a quick gulp of air either forward or sideways just as the arms begin to pull. It is faster to swim the breaststroke under the water, but in competitive breaststroke the head must break the surface at some point in each stroke cycle except for the first complete stroke cycle off the wall. On the start and in the turn, therefore, breaststrokers take advantage of this rule by pushing off into an arm-extended prone glide under water— pulling the arms all the way through to the sides of the body, gliding again, and then kicking to the surface to resume stroking. The breaststroke turn is done by grabbing the wall with both hands parallel and simultaneously tucking the body up and pushing off in a prone glide, arms extended overhead (fig. 10.2).

The competitive butterfly stroke is the same as described in chapter 6. Since this stroke requires a great deal of energy, much practice and conditioning is needed before a swimmer can race with it. Since both hands must touch the wall simultaneously in both the breaststroke and butterfly strokes, the same kind of turn is performed.

Another race of interest is the individual medley. In this event, the competitor swims one quarter of the distance using each of the strokes in the following order: butterfly, backstroke, breaststroke, and free-style. To win at this event, you must be an excellent all-around swimmer.

Relay races are a part of every swimming meet. In these events, four swimmers combine into a team, each swimming one quarter of the required distance. In the free-style relay, each of the team members swims free-style. In the medley relay, the first swimmer swims backstroke, the second breaststroke, the third butterfly, and the fourth or "anchor" swims free-style.

How does the competitive breaststroke differ from the conventional breaststroke?

Competitive Diving

In competitive diving, the performer is required to execute dives from five different categories: forward, backward, reverse, inward, and twisting. The selection and number of dives done are determined by the level of the meet and the skill of the participants.

In the forward dive category, the diver takes an approach and hurdle, then dives forward into the water. The dive may contain any number of somersaults with either a headfirst or feetfirst entry. Additional turns may be added up to and including three and one-half somersaults. Obviously the more difficult dives are the ones with the most somersaults.

In backward dives the performer stands with his or her back to the water, toes on the end of the board, and dives backwards into the pool. Since no hurdle is taken, height must be attained by a single press of the board. Here again, somersaults are added to increase difficulty.

If the diver walks forward on the board and takes a hurdle but then dives backward into the water, he or she is performing a reverse dive, sometimes improperly called a "gainer." Board control and proper hurdle position are critical, but when properly performed, the reverse dive can be one of the most artistic and eye appealing movements in diving.

The inward dive is the opposite of the reverse dive. The performer stands backwards as in the back dive, but as he or she is propelled up and away by the spring of the board, the performer dives forward in the direction of the board. This dive also requires good board technique and may include any number of somersaults.

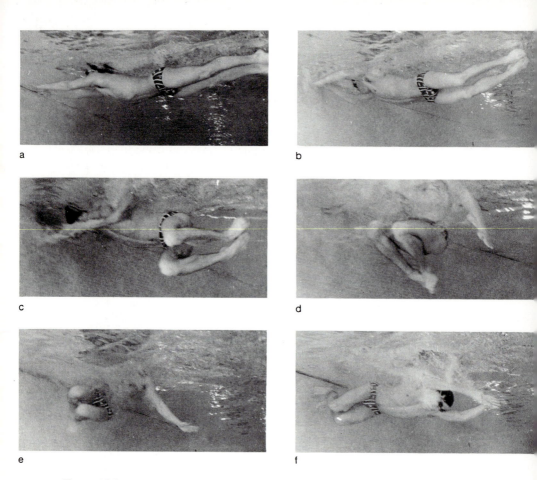

a

b

c

d

e

f

Figure 10.2
The breaststroke turn.

When the diver adds a twisting action, or a turn around the long axis of the body, while performing any of the previously mentioned dives, he or she is executing a twisting dive. These dives are usually considered more difficult than similar dives in other categories because they require two actions—both a somersaulting and a twisting action. On twist dives, difficulty is determined by the number of somersaults and the number of twists. Two of the most difficult of all dives are the triple twisting forward one and one-half somersault and the double twisting forward two and one-half somersault.

In addition to these categories of dives, the diver may elect to perform a dive in any one of three body positions—the tuck, the pike, or the straight position. Some dives allow a "free" position which means the diver may perform more than one position during the progress of the dive. In any case, the straight body or layout position should be assumed on entry to assure a minimum of splash.

Judges grade a dive on the form (body posture, toes pointed, knees straight), the approach and hurdle, height, technique and control, and the entry (body position and amount of splash). They give a score ranging from zero to ten in half-point increments. The scorekeepers then multiply the composite judges score by the degree of difficulty of the dive to determine its final point value.

Diving usually takes place on springboards which are 1 or 3 meters off the water, but in high level competition, platform diving is contested from heights as far above the water as 10 meters. Olympic competition consists of 3-meter springboard and 10-meter platform events.

Hints for Speeding Up Progress

11

Swimming, like most sport activities, is complicated and you will need many hours of practice to perfect the various strokes. For most rapid learning, you should take advantage of a course taught by a qualified instructor. Learning by yourself or copying others is not only difficult, but may lead to bad habits that are hard to break when you later want to learn correctly.

In addition to the expert instruction which a qualified teacher can provide, regular practice sessions are required. Distributed practice is superior to massed practice when learning complicated skills that require long periods of time to master. The two or three times per week that your class meets helps to provide this arrangement. In addition to the class time, you will probably have to do a little "homework" on your own to progress at your most rapid rate.

When in class, pay close attention to what the instructor says and make every effort to do as he or she indicates. The instructor has taught many people to swim and has found certain techniques that help beginners learn quickly. When you practice on your own time, don't just play in the water. Work on the specific points that were mentioned in class. Do some of the drills and exercises that you know will help you. Remember that it will take a conscious effort to overcome fears and to learn new skills such as rhythmic breathing and coordinated movements of the arms, legs, and head. Mere exposure to the water and horseplay with friends will not teach you how to swim.

Another important factor in speeding up your progress is an understanding of the scientific principles which relate to the human body in motion. A study of these factors called "kinesiology." Several of these factors are very important in swimming. Knowledge of them, and proper application of techniques dictated by these principles, can make you a better swimmer. The three most important concepts from kinesiology that relate to swimming are: flotation (Archimedes' principle), Newton's third law of motion (action and reaction), and resistance or drag in the water.

Archimedes' Principle

This principle is very important to the swimmer. Since your body is buoyed up by the forces equal to the weight of the amount of water you displace, it is obvious that you receive more buoyancy if you keep more of your body under water. (See page 14 for a definition of Archimedes' principle) The head is the most dense (no pun intended) part of your body. Hence, if you lift it out of the water, you will lose buoyancy, and the weight of your head will force your body under water. This is one of the most common errors committed by beginning swimmers. To take full advantage of buoyancy, it would be ideal to keep your whole head under water at all times. Obviously, this is not possible because it is necessary to breathe occasionally! You should therefore adjust the position of your head so that it is as low as possible in the water, yet held in a position so that with a minimum of rotation, the nose and mouth can be raised above the surface of the water for inhalation. Refer to the discussion of breathing on the crawl stroke in chapter 6 for a description of proper head position.

When this position is attained, and a reasonable speed is maintained through the water, a wave of water is built up in front of the head, and the trough from that wave is formed by the side of the head. With practice you can learn to turn your head and breathe the air that is in the trough which is actually slightly below the surface of the surrounding water. This technique is very helpful as it allows the head to remain low in the water to take maximum advantage of the buoyancy effect. Rolling the head for breathing is the correct method, lifting the head out of the water is the incorrect method. Lifting the head results in loss of the buoyancy effect, lowers the legs, and places the chest in a frontal position in the water, thus increasing resistance to forward motion.

Newton's Third Law (Action and Reaction)

Newton's principle applied to swimming states: when water is forced backward by either the arms or the legs, the resultant reaction will propel the body forward. Hence, to increase force and speed in swimming, your actions should be designed to push the water straight backwards, and not to the side, up, or down. This means that the arm stroke should proceed in a line with the body, and not push the water down (which would tend to raise the body above the water) or sidewards (which would be wasted effort in our attempts to move forward). The "S" pattern of the arm stroke for the crawl described in chapter 6 is not designed to push water sideways, but rather to allow the swimmer to bend the elbow slightly so that the resistance arm is shortened, thus reducing the effort needed to complete the stroke.

The leg kick also provides a propelling force to drive the swimmer through the water. In the frog, whip, and scissors kick, the squeezing action of the legs forces water toward the feet of the swimmer and thus results in a forward movement of the body.

In the flutter kick, the action-reaction process is more complicated. The flutter kick is composed of three phases: 1) the knee bend, 2) the knee extension, and 3) the lift of the entire leg from the hip. Review chapter 4 for a description of the flutter kick.

Phase one actually produces a negative effect on the forward propulsion of the body, but is necessary to prepare for the positive effects of phases two and three (fig. 11.1).

Figure 11.1
Phase one of the flutter kick: the knee bend.

Note that the water is actually driven forward, which forces the body backward slightly.

Phase two involves extension of the knee joint and forces some of the water backward, which produces a slight forward propulsion of the body (fig. 11.2).

Figure 11.2
Phase two of the flutter kick: the knee extension.

Phase three is the most powerful part of the flutter kick as it involves the entire leg and forces more water backwards, thus producing more forward drive. This is the ''up'' part of the kick described in chapter 4 and is the part that should be emphasized most since it produces the most forward drive (fig. 11.3).

Figure 11.3
Phase three of the flutter kick: the lift from the hip.

Which kinesiological principles are illustrated by each of the following swimming movements: stroking the arms in a line with the body, recovering the arms above water, and carrying the head as low as possible in the water?

Resistance or Drag in the Water

This third principle from kinesiology is the most obvious one of all. The less surface area presented as the body glides through the water, the less will be the resistance or ''drag'' on the body. The body in a straight line, with the arms extended in front of the head or at the sides, is in the most efficient position for gliding through the water. When you lift your head from the water, not only do you lose buoyancy, but the movement tends to lower the legs, arch the back, and present the chest and abdominal area as a surface to be driven through the water. Because the chest and abdominal area are a greater surface area that must be pushed through the water, this is an inefficient position for gliding (fig. 11.4).

Another technique that reduces drag is the recovery of the arms above the water on most strokes. For example, in the crawl, the arms pull under the water, and then recover above the water. This makes the stroke more efficient.

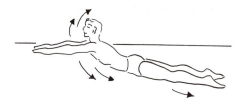

Figure 11.4
Resistance or drag in the water.

But if you drag your arms or fingers through the water on the recovery phase of the arm stroke, you will increase resistance and slow down your speed. The whip kick is more efficient than the frog kick for a similar reason. On the preparatory phase of the whip kick, there is less drag in the water than there is in the same phase of the frog kick.

If you understand the principles described above, you will not only improve your swimming efficiency, but you will be able to analyze your own errors and correct them based on your knowledge of the principles. The scientific application of the principles of physics to swimming and other sports is one of the major contributions of the modern study of kinesiology within the field of physical education.

While learning the elementary backstroke, beginners sometimes drop their hips on the leg recovery or lift the hands above the surface on the arm recovery. Explain the effect of each of these mistakes in terms of the appropriate kinesiological concept.

When you have mastered the techniques of the various strokes, you will want to develop some speed and endurance in the water. To develop your speed, you must use the correct technique and force yourself to swim fast for 25 or 50 yards. Swim repeat 50 yard distances with about thirty seconds rest between each one. Start with two, then build to three, four, even ten in a row.

To develop endurance, aim at being able to swim a quarter mile (440 yards), or more. Start with 100 yards and increase the distance by 25 or 50 yards each week. Be sure to utilize correct breathing and body position. Minimize any extreme motion such as too much body roll, movement of the trunk sideways, or excessive head action. Relax and change strokes occasionally in order to utilize different muscle groups. Force yourself to keep going when you begin to get tired. Your cardiovascular system can't improve unless you make it work. Once you have made a quarter of a mile, the half and full mile are easy. If you would like to enter competitive swimming, see a coach for more specific workout schedules or have your teacher set up a workout plan for you.

References

You can find additional information about swimming, diving, and related aquatic sports activities in the following books and journals:

Books

American Alliance for Health, Physical Education, Recreation and Dance. *In The Pool (Swimming for the Disabled).* Reston, Va: American Alliance for Health, Physical Education, Recreation and Dance, 1985.

American Red Cross. *Swimming and Diving.* St. Louis: C. V. Mosby Co., 1992.

Armbruster, David A.; Allen, Robert H.; and Billingsley, Hobert S. *Swimming and Diving.* 7th ed. St. Louis: C. V. Mosby Co., 1979.

Ballatore, Ron; Miller, William; and O'Connor, Bob. *Swimming and Aquatics Today.* St. Paul: West Publishing Co., 1990.

Casten, Carole. *Aqua Aerobics Today.* St. Paul: West Publishing Co., 1991.

Colwin, Cecil M. *Swimming into the 21st Century.* Champaign, Il: Leisure Press, 1992.

Costil, David L.; Maglischo, Ernest W.; and Richardson, Allen B. *Swimming (Handbook of Sports Medicine and Science).* Champaign, Il: Leisure Press, 1992.

Forbes, Margaret Swan. *Coaching Synchronized Swimming Effectively.* Champaign, Il: Human Kinetics Pub., 1989.

Jones, Michael H. *The ABC's of Swimming.* Dubuque, Ia: Kendall/Hunt Pub. Co., 1990.

Larrabee, Jean G. *Coaching Swimming Effectively.* Champaign, Il: Human Kinetics Pub., 1992.

Leonard, John, ed. *Science of Coaching Swimming.* Champaign, Il: Leisure Press, 1992.

Maglischo, Ernest W. *Swimming Faster: A Comprehensive Guide to the Science of Swimming.* Mountain View, Ca: Mayfield Pub. Co., 1992.

Maglischo, Ernest W., and Brennan, Cathy Ferguson. *Swim for the Health of It.* Mountain View, Ca: Mayfield Pub. Co., 1992.

Messner, Yvonne J., and Assmann, Nikki. *Swimming Everyone.* Winston Salem, NC: Hunter Textbooks, Inc., 1989.

O'Brien, Ron. *Diving for Gold.* Champaign, Il: Leisure Press, 1992.

Sova, Ruth. *Aquatics, The Complete Reference Guide for Aquatic Fitness Professionals.* Boston: Jones and Bartlett Pub., 1991, 302pp.

Sova, Ruth. *Aquatics Exercise.* Boston: Jones and Bartlett Pub., 1992.

Thomas, David G. *Advanced Swimming— Steps to Success.* Champaign, Il: Leisure Press, 1990.

U. S. Swimming News: The Official Newsletter of United States Swimming. Colorado Springs, Co: 1750 E. Boulder, 80909–5770.

Vickers, Betty J. *Fundamentals of Springboard Diving.* Boston: American Press, 1989.

YMCA of the USA. *Aquatics for Special Populations.* Champaign Il: Human Kinetics Pub., 1992.

Journals

Journal of Physical Education, Recreation and Dance. Reston, Va: American Alliance for Health, Physical Education, Recreation and Dance.

Journal of Swimming Research. Fort Lauderdale, Fl: American Swimming Coaches Association in cooperation with the United States Swimming's Sports Medicine Committee.

Swimming Technique. Los Angeles: P. O. Box 45497.

Swimming World. Los Angeles: P. O. Box 45497.

Questions and Answers

Multiple Choice

1. When performing the flutter kick with the front crawl, the knees should be
   a. nearly straight and relaxed.
   b. bent at about forty-five degrees.
   c. bent on the upstroke and straight on the downstroke.
   d. bent at about fifteen degrees. (p. 30)
2. When performing the flutter kick with the back crawl, you should
   a. kick from the knees.
   b. flex the ankles.
   c. emphasize the up kick.
   d. alternately flex and extend your ankles. (p. 31)
3. The flutter kick should originate from
   a. the hip joint.
   b. the knee joint.
   c. the lower back.
   d. the ankle joint. (p. 37)
4. When performing the front crawl, the arms should be
   a. bent ninety degrees when under the water.
   b. bent slightly when under the water.
   c. straight when above the water.
   d. straight at all times. (p. 38)
5. In the front crawl stroke, if breathing on the left side, a good method of coordinating the arm stroke and the breathing is to
   a. inhale as you lift your right arm.
   b. turn your face toward your left arm as the pull is completed.
   c. rest your head on your right arm.
   d. keep your head out of the water. (p. 37)
6. In the front crawl stroke, if breathing is to the left side, while the right arm is out of the water, the swimmer should be
   a. inhaling.
   b. exhaling.
   c. holding his or her breath.
   d. looking to his or her right. (p. 37)
7. The phase of the whip kick that propels the swimmer through the water is the
   a. apart phase.
   b. recovery stage.
   c. glide phase.
   d. press phase. (p. 35)

8. During the whip kick, the thighs should
   a. not be rotated.
   b. be rotated inward.
   c. be rotated downward.
   d. be rotated outward. (p. 36)
9. In the elementary backstroke, the
   a. arms pull first.
   b. legs kick first.
   c. arms and legs press simultaneously.
   d. none of these. (p. 35)
10. In the elementary backstroke, the arms
    a. extend slightly above the head.
    b. extend directly to the side.
    c. are bent when they pull.
    d. pull deep into the water. (p. 36)
11. One of the most common errors committed by beginners when performing the back float is
    a. keeping the head in line with the body.
    b. keeping their hips up.
    c. sitting in the water.
    d. relaxing. (p. 30)
12. In the breaststroke, after the glide,
    a. the arms pull before the legs kick.
    b. the legs kick before the arms pull.
    c. the arms and legs work together.
    d. you breathe as the legs kick. (p. 44)
13. In the breaststroke
    a. the arms extend forward, beyond the head.
    b. the arms pull and touch the sides of the body.
    c. the arms come out of the water.
    d. the arms glide at the sides of the body. (p. 44)
14. The common factor in the elementary backstroke and the breaststroke that makes them relatively low-energy strokes is the
    a. arm pull.
    b. leg kick.
    c. position in the water.
    d. glide. (pp. 35, 44)
15. To what does the term ''sculling'' refer?
    a. a form of sailboat racing
    b. traveling headfirst through the water
    c. a method of propelling your body, using just your hands and arms
    d. a method of propelling your body, using just your feet (p. 30)
16. When doing the back crawl, how are the arms placed in the water?
    a. elbow first
    b. little finger first
    c. back of hand first
    d. thumb first (p. 40)

17. Aside from lying on your back, the inverted breaststroke is the same as the conventional breaststroke except for the breathing and
    a. kick.
    b. arm action.
    c. head turn.
    d. knee bend. (p. 46)
18. Which of the following best describes the scissors kick?
    a. top leg goes forward
    b. legs split forward and backward
    c. bottom leg goes downward
    d. swimmer lies on his or her side in the water (p. 42)
19. When swimming the American crawl, the recommended number of flutter kicks to be performed during one complete arm cycle is
    a. two.
    b. four.
    c. six.
    d. eight. (p. 35)
20. When swimming the front crawl, which of the following best describes the correct head position. The water level during exhalation should coincide with the swimmer's
    a. eyes.
    b. chin.
    c. nose.
    d. hairline. (p. 39)
21. When performing the tuck surface dive, which of the following is true?
    a. Knees are bent, hips are straight.
    b. Knees are straight, hips are bent.
    c. Knees are straight, hips are straight.
    d. Knees are bent, hips are bent. (p. 60)
22. Which of the following best describes the timing and rhythm of the breaststroke?
    a. pull, kick, breathe, glide
    b. kick, pull, breathe, glide
    c. kick, breathe, pull, glide
    d. pull and breathe, kick, glide (p. 45)
23. When performing the flutter kick in a supine position, one should emphasize mostly the
    a. up kick.
    b. down kick.
    c. knee bend.
    d. hip flexion. (p. 40)
24. In the front crawl, the head is turned to the side to breathe so that
    a. stroke rhythm will not be interrupted.
    b. the mouth can come completely out of the water.
    c. the head will continue to be buoyed up by the water.
    d. you can both inhale and exhale while the mouth is out of the water. (p. 39)

25. Which of the following best describes the difference between the scissors kick and the whip kick?
    a. less thrust in scissors kick
    b. longer glide in whip kick
    c. a lateral leg action is used in the scissors kick
    d. a lateral leg action is used in the whip kick.   (pp. 35, 45–46)
26. In the breaststroke, it is important to begin the exhalation before the head is raised so that
    a. stroke rhythm will not be interrupted.
    b. the exhalation will assist in providing thrust.
    c. the glide will be enhanced.
    d. specific gravity will be reduced.   (p. 46)
27. In which of the following strokes is it possible to inhale during the glide phase?
    a. elementary backstroke
    b. front crawl
    c. back crawl
    d. breaststroke   (p. 40)
28. When performing the back crawl, the arms should
    a. be bent at the elbow when recovering.
    b. pull diagonally to the water surface.
    c. pull perpendicular to the water surface.
    d. pull as deep in the water as possible.   (p. 40)
29. When performing the sidestroke with your left side down, your right arm pushes as
    a. your left arm pulls.
    b. you breathe.
    c. your legs squeeze together.
    d. you glide.   (p. 44)
30. During the approach phase of the dive, the hurdle step should be
    a. twenty-four inches long.
    b. on the same spot as the last step.
    c. the same distance as two of the diver's normal walking steps.
    d. the same distance as one of the diver's normal walking steps.   (p. 57)
31. Which of the following is the most efficient kick to use when treading water?
    a. flutter
    b. dolphin
    c. scissors or whip
    d. trudgen   (p. 32)
32. The principle of buoyancy was discovered by
    a. Bernouli.
    b. Archimedes.
    c. Einstein.
    d. Plank.   (pp. 14, 28)
33. In the front crawl, which of the following best describes the correct placement of the arm or hand in the water?
    a. little finger first
    b. elbow first
    c. fingertips first
    d. palm first   (p. 37)

True or False

34. Proper technique in the inverted breaststroke includes the whip kick. (p. 48)
35. The butterfly stroke, because of its difficulty, is one of the slowest strokes in competitive swimming. (p. 48)
36. The breathing method in the butterfly stroke may be to the side or directly forward. (p. 50)
37. After learning to swim, one may swim alone safely. (p. 5)
38. The whip kick is similar to the frog kick except for a difference in position of the knees and feet. (p. 35)
39. A sculling action of the hands should be used when treading water. (p. 32)
40. If you can prove you are an expert swimmer, you may swim alone. (p. 2)
41. Even though you may not know the exact way to rescue a person, you should do your best to swim to that person to save him or her. (p. 7)
42. The crawl is commonly referred to as the "free-style" in competitive swimming. (p. 37)
43. The American crawl is usually performed with one complete arm stroke of both arms to six kicks of the legs. (p. 37)
44. The flutter kick should originate primarily from the knees with your legs relaxed, and the kick breaking the surface of the water. (p. 37)
45. In the butterfly stroke, there are usually two leg kicks to each arm cycle. (p. 48)
46. The four competitive speed swimming strokes are the free-style, back crawl, elementary backstroke, and the breaststroke. (p. 64)
47. The kick used in the sidestroke is the scissors kick. (p. 42)
48. The sidestroke, elementary backstroke, and breaststroke all begin and end in a glide. (pp. 35, 42, 44)
49. The breathing method in the breaststroke is the same as that in the front crawl. (pp. 39, 46)
50. When first learning how to dive, begin in a kneeling position off the side of the low board. (p. 57)
51. The sidestroke is considered to be a racing stroke. (p. 42)
52. The whip kick should be used in the elementary backstroke and the breaststroke. (pp. 35, 44)
53. There is a glide phase in the free-style and backstroke when one arm is extended above the head and the other arm is down to the side. (pp. 35, 37)
54. The back crawl is the fastest stroke one can swim because of the continuous pull of the arms and the kick of the feet. (p. 39)
55. To be considered safe in deep water, you must be able to jump into the water, level off the body, and proceed with a stroke. (p. 55)
56. Four types of surface dives are tuck, pike, feetfirst, and swim-down. (pp. 60, 61)
57. When treading water, the most important thing to remember is to keep your head and shoulders up to avoid getting water in the face. (p. 32)
58. In competitive diving, the legal approach consists of at least two steps and a hurdle. (p. 57)
59. The "jackknife" is officially described as the front dive in pike position. (p. 57)
60. It has been estimated that forty percent of all persons who are drowned yearly are school-aged children. (p. 3)
61. Swimming, diving, and other water games are good natural outlets for one's competitive drive. (p. 3)

62. Swimming is considered very dangerous for mentally and physically handicapped persons because the likelihood of their drowning is extremely high. (p. 3)
63. One drawback to swimming is the lack of pools and other suitable places due to expense. (p. 2)
64. The primary purpose of learning to swim is to be able to swim well enough to compete if desired. (p. 1)
65. Fear of water often is the result of an unfortunate incident that occurred in the early learning stages of the beginning swimmer. (p. 19)
66. The initial shock of cold water on your body may tense your muscles; therefore, don't completely submerge at first. Rather, stand knee deep and splash water on the other parts of your body. (p. 19)
67. Breath control, which is necessary for maximum success in water activities, is easy to develop. (p. 20)
68. It is a bad habit to wipe your face and eyes with your hands after submerging, for it will inhibit your progress later on. (p. 20)
69. Bobbing is a rhythmic breathing method helpful in learning breath control. (p. 21)
70. The type of rhythmic breathing method used in the crawl stroke is that which is learned from the side of the pool—start face down in the water, turn your face to the side to inhale, and back down again to exhale. (p. 22)
71. A nonswimmer should not in any manner try to rescue a drowning person. (p. 7)
72. The flutter kick is used in the front and back crawl. (pp. 37, 40)
73. The only two types of floating are the jellyfish float and the prone float. (pp. 28, 29)
74. Any swimming arm stroke is composed of a catch, pull, and recovery movement. (pp. 35, 36, 40, 44, 46, 48)
75. When performing the breaststroke, the arms should be pulled all the way to the hip. (p. 44)
76. In the breaststroke, when the arms are extended forward and in front of the head, the legs are extended to the rear. (p. 46)
77. Whenever possible, a swimming type rescue should be used to save a drowning person. (p. 7)
78. A pike position in diving means that the hips are bent and the knees are straight. (p. 60)
79. The tuck position is commonly called the ''jackknife.'' (p. 59)
80. Regular workouts are essential to maintain fitness through swimming. (p. 67)
81. Competitive sprint swimmers breathe on every stroke of the arms. (p. 70)
82. In competitive diving, the performer is required to execute dives from five different categories. (pp. 70, 71)
83. When a diver adds a twist, it usually increases the difficulty of the dive. (p. 72)
84. A ''gainer'' is more properly called an inward dive. (p. 71)
85. Three body positions in diving are tuck, pike, and straight. (p. 72)
86. A medley race includes four different strokes. (pp. 69, 70)
87. Most swimming rules are designed to make the sport more safe and more enjoyable. (p. 5)
88. A flip turn is used in free-style sprint races. (p. 71)
89. The word SCUBA is an abbreviation for self-contained underwater breathing apparatus. (p. 65)
90. Man is known to have participated in swimming at least as early as 2000 B.C. (p. 13)

Matching

	Term		Stroke
91.	Head turned to side for breathing	(p. 24)	A. Front crawl
92.	Flutter kick	(pp. 23, 24)	B. Back crawl
93.	Straight arm recovery	(p. 39)	C. Elementary back
94.	Recovery, power, glide rhythm	(p. 35)	D. Breast
95.	Emphasis on the up kick	(p. 40)	E. Side
96.	Scissors kick	(p. 42)	
97.	Fastest stroke	(p. 37)	
98.	Arms and legs press simultaneously	(p. 35)	
99.	Pull and breathe, kick, glide, rhythm	(p. 44)	
100.	Whip kick	(pp. 44, 46)	

Question Answer Key

Multiple Choice

1. a	8. a	15. c	22. d	29. c
2. c	9. c	16. b	23. a	30. d
3. a	10. a	17. b	24. c	31. c
4. b	11. c	18. b	25. d	32. b
5. b	12. a	19. c	26. a	33. c
6. b	13. a	20. d	27. a	
7. d	14. d	21. d	28. b	

True or False

34. T	46. F	58. F	70. T	82. T
35. F	47. T	59. T	71. F	83. T
36. T	48. T	60. T	72. T	84. F
37. F	49. F	61. T	73. F	85. T
38. T	50. F	62. F	74. T	86. T
39. T	51. F	63. F	75. F	87. T
40. F	52. T	64. F	76. T	88. T
41. F	53. F	65. T	77. F	89. T
42. T	54. F	66. T	78. T	90. T
43. T	55. T	67. F	79. F	
44. F	56. T	68. T	80. T	
45. T	57. F	69. T	81. F	

Matching

91. A	96. E
92. A, B	97. A
93. B	98. C
94. C	99. D
95. B	100. C, D

Index

SCUBA. *See* Self-contained underwater breathing apparatus (SCUBA)
skin. *See* Skin diving
stationary, 56–57
surface, 60–61
Dolphin kick, 48–49
defined, 15
Drag, 75, 77–78
defined, 16
Drugs, 8, 11

Eating, 6
Egypt, 13
Electric shock, 8, 11
Elementary backstroke, 35–37
England, 13
Entering, 19
Entry, 39
Equipment, and facilities, 4

Facilities, and equipment, 4
Finning, 31–32
defined, 15
First aid, 9
Flip turn, 51, 53
Float, defined, 15
Floating, 27–34
Flop, back, 58
Flotation, 75–76
Flotation device, 5–6, 16, 63
See also Personal flotation device (PFD)
Flutter kick, 23–24, 30–31, 37, 40, 76–77
defined, 15
Flying Gull, 13
Footfirst dive, 60–61
Forward approach and hurdle. *See* Approach and hurdle
Forward dive, in pike position, 57–58
Free position, and diving, 72
Freestyle, 37, 69, 71
Front crawl stroke, 37–39

Gainer, 71
Glide, 29, 30–31, 35, 42, 46
defined, 15
Go, and rescue, 7–8
Goose pimples, 19
Grab turn, 50
Gutter, defined, 15

Hazards, 4
Heart attack, 8, 11
History, 13–14
Human chain, 7
Hurdle. *See* Approach and hurdle

Indians, 13
Individual medley, 71
Inhale, 45
Instructor, 5
Intermediate swimmer, and conditioning, 68
Inverted breaststroke, 46–48

Jackknife, 57–58
Journals, 80
Jumping, and diving, 55–56

Kick, 42, 46, 76, 77
defined, 15
See also specific kicks
Kickboard, 21, 23, 24
Knee bend, 76–77
Knee extension, 76–77

Leveling off, 55, 56
Lift, from hip, 76–77
Longfellow, Wilbert E., 14

Medley, individual, 71
Motion. *See* Newton's Third Law of Motion
Mouth-to-mouth resuscitation, 8, 9–10
defined, 15

Natatorium, defined, 15
Neutral buoyancy, 28
Newton's Third Law of Motion, 38, 75, 76–77
defined, 16
New York Athletic Club, 13
Nonswimmer
and beginning techniques, 19–25
and conditioning, 67–68
Novice, and conditioning, 67

Personal flotation device (PFD), defined, 16
PFD. *See* Personal flotation device (PFD)
Physiological values, 1–2
Pike, 57–58, 60
defined, 16
surface dive, 60–61
Planting feet, 70
Pollution, 4
Polo. *See* Water polo
Pompeii, 13
Power, 35
Pressing, 68
Prone float, 29, 30–31, 32, 33
defined, 15
Prone glide, 29, 30–31
Pull, 39, 42, 46
defined, 16